Daily Mail
BUYING A HOME ABROAD
1990

Daily Mail
BUYING A HOME ABROAD 1990

REBECCA STEPHENS

SIDGWICK & JACKSON
LONDON

The author and publishers would like to thank Diana Wildman, who writes about international property purchasing for The Times, *for her valuable comments on the manuscript.*

Maps by John Flower

First published in 1989 by Sidgwick & Jackson Limited
1 Tavistock Chambers, Bloomsbury Way
London WC1A 2SG

Copyright © 1989 by Rebecca Stephens

All rights reserved. No part of this
publication may be reproduced, stored in a
retrieval system, or transmitted in any form
or by any means, electronic, mechanical,
photocopying, recording or otherwise,
without the written permission of the
copyright owner.

ISBN 0 283 99826 1

Typeset by Hewer Text Composition Services, Edinburgh
Printed by Billing & Sons Limited, Worcester
for Sidgwick & Jackston Limited

CONTENTS

Introduction		7
1	France	13
2	Italy	29
3	Mainland Spain	38
4	The Balearics	52
5	Canary Islands	63
6	Portugal	73
7	Greece	81
8	Cyprus	89
9	Turkey	95
10	Malta	104
11	Andorra	112
12	Ireland	118
13	Ski Resorts	123
14	Costs	140
List of Property Agents		149
List of Embassies		159
Acknowledgements		160

INTRODUCTION

Buying a home abroad is an attractive, rather extravagant idea that has appealed to most of us at one time or another, and yet only a few years ago it was considered possible only for the privileged few. It wasn't so many years ago, though, that travel, particularly air travel, was thought exciting, adventurous, even glamorous; now it's rather mundane. Motorways, electrified railways and most of all the passenger jet have made the world a smaller place, opening up huge opportunities not just for holidays abroad, but also for that dream of buying a home in the sun, or on the ski slopes, whichever is your choice. Many not-so-privileged people have already grasped that opportunity: the number of foreigners who have bought property in Spain alone runs into millions.

Sigmund Freud is said to have remarked that the really big decisions in life – who and when to marry, for instance, or which house to buy – should be taken on the spur of the moment: it's the less important matters that are worth mulling over. He may well have been right. Certainly, how you feel instinctively about a house has a lot of bearing on whether or not you will buy it. It might be prudent, however, when buying a home abroad to throw his remark to the wind – or, at least, to classify a home abroad, in his phraseology, as a 'less important matter'.

There are a few questions you should ask yourself before embarking on making your overseas investment. The attractions are obvious: a place abroad you can call your own, where you can do your own thing, pop over for the odd week or even weekends, and share with family and friends. But what about the expense, the running costs and upkeep? You could argue that you could let it out – that, at least, should cover the costs in part – besides which you will be *saving* money, perhaps hundreds of pounds a year on extravagant holidays elsewhere. But what about the worry, the sheer hassle of looking after a property in a foreign country? Well, that's a point. You could, though, hand it over to a management company. At the end of the day, you will weigh up the pros and cons and decide one way or another. If you go ahead, what is certain is that you will be buying an adventure, and, if you choose carefully, a sound, even lucrative investment. A few practical points, though, should be kept in mind:

Where to buy

You may already have decided that the only possible property for you is a rambling farmhouse in the Tuscan hills, or a chalet in the Savoie Alps, in which case your research need go no further. If, however, your only wish is for a villa in the sun, whether it be Greek, Spanish or Portuguese sun, then you should make a few enquiries before deciding on a location. A two-week holiday, or even several two-week holidays, in a resort isn't enough if you intend to use the property off-season; it certainly isn't enough if you intend to retire there. You should check out local amenities, local restaurants and shopping facilities. Are they open out of season? What character does the resort take on when the sun doesn't shine? To answer your questions there is no substitute for talking to people, getting as much disinterested advice as you can from locals and from other foreigners who know the area well. Nothing is more depressing than a lively, vibrant development that turns into a dreary 'ghost urbanization' in winter months. It doesn't make much sense for letting, either.

Accessibility is another point to consider. It goes without saying that the more you intend to use your home abroad, the easier it should be to get to. Impromptu weekends can be ruled out if a four-hour drive awaits you on landing at the airport.

Agents and inspection trips

You have no doubt heard the saying 'let the buyer beware'; this is certainly true when buying a property abroad. The prospective purchaser of a holiday home in the sun makes an attractive target for the dishonest or simply pushy agent, hungry for his commission.

Once again, word of mouth is probably the most satisfactory route to finding a reputable and helpful agent, well established in the sales of overseas property. Otherwise, there are a couple of recognized associations that set out to protect the interests of the public. The National Association of Estate Agents and FOPDAC, the Federation of Overseas Property Developers, Agents and Consultants, both enforce strict codes of practice on their associate members.

Many agents and developers lay on inspection trips, a chance for you to view or even stay in properties they have on offer. Some offer the opportunity to travel at reduced rates or even free of charge, or else they may offer a complete refund of the costs in the event of a purchase. Beware, though, that in a real world there is no such thing as a free lunch, as the saying goes, or, indeed, a subsidized inspection trip. For every two prospective buyers who actually make a purchase, another eight may not. The cost of these long weekends in the sun has to be covered somehow – usually in the purchase price of the property, even if indirectly through higher marketing costs and agency fees.

By all means make use of inspection trips – the additional cost of one extra body won't make so much difference, after all – but don't be pressurized into paying a deposit then and there and, most importantly, don't sign anything when you first meet the builder or developer. If you do feel pressurized into paying a deposit, make sure it is returnable if you change your mind. Ideally you should return home with full specifications and a plan of the property, plus a copy of the contract in English so that you can refer it to your solicitor. Remember, you can always make a return trip under your own steam and view the development, and other developments, in your own time.

The legal side

The only question you need ask yourself here is would you buy a house in England without consulting a solicitor? The answer, surely, is *no*, unless you decided to employ a registered conveyancer, or embarked on the DIY approach, studying the relevant books and finding out exactly what was involved. And yet every year thousands of investors happily part with their hard-earned savings to buy a property abroad without consulting a lawyer; and many of these purchasers have little or no knowledge of the varying rules and customs, even the language, in their chosen country. So every year there are horror stories in the press of people who have lost money buying houses which don't exist, or are unfinished, or belong to someone else.

Although such unfortunate events undoubtedly hit the headlines, and in reality form a small proportion of the total number of transactions in any one year, the message is clear: don't be one of the gullible few –

INTERNATIONAL ESTATE AGENTS

ITALY · GREECE · CYPRUS · FRANCE · TURKEY ·

Brian A. French & Associates have specialised in the Italian Property market for over fifteen years and are respected worldwide. Throughout UMBRIA, TUSCANY and LE MARCHE we offer the widest selection of
• Cottages • Farmhouses • Castles • Palaces • Farms • Vineyards • Investments. Through our network we can also locate specific investments in other regions on request.

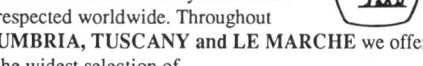

Whiteway Properties is an established agency with exclusive contacts in the above countries and is the sole agent for the highly respected P Cassimatis Organisation based in Athens. Every type of freehold is available from a small holiday apartment to a complete hotel complex and development projects. We can also assist in locating other types of related investments in these, and other regions..

Our fully comprehensive Service includes:
Initial Advice, Inspection Visits, Assistance with Purchase Procedures and International Banking, Building Restoration Services, After Sales Care

Your FREE copy of our current Overseas Property News and Italian Property Guide are obtainable from our offices by 'phoning, writing or calling.

BRIAN A FRENCH & ASSOCIATES LTD and WHITEWAY PROPERTIES
SUITES 2 - 3, 12 High Street, Knaresborough, North Yorkshire.Telephone: (0423) 865892/867047
Fax: (0423) 863755 and in London Telephone: 01 485 8466 Fax: 01 485 4852

Members of the: National Association of Estate Agents
FIABCI - The International Real Estate Federation. The Federation of Overseas Property Developers Agents and Consultants
The Italian Chamber of Commerce & The Anglo Turkish Business Council

employ a lawyer. Your solicitor should be able to recommend a specialist firm who can instruct a lawyer in the country where you plan to buy. Alternatively, the relevant embassy in London or your agent may be able to help.

Before signing a purchase contract or handing over any money, check with your lawyer that he has carried out a full and thorough search on the property. Most important of all is the title. It is quite common, for instance, for a property abroad, particularly for an old rural property, to be jointly owned by several members of a family; all must give their consent if the sale is to go ahead. Your solicitor should also check there are no outstanding debts assigned to the property, and that it was built with the necessary planning permission from the local authorities.

If you are buying off-plan or before a property has been completed, it's worth making a thorough investigation into the financial credibility of the agent or developer you are dealing with. In Spain, developers are legally bound to offer buyers a guarantee of completion backed by a bank or other financial institution. Your lawyer should also check the area immediately surrounding your property – whether, for instance, there are plans to construct a new road or, worse still, a high-rise block of flats that might have serious consequences on both the aesthetic and financial value of your property.

These are a few general points to consider. Specific information concerning each country is given in detail in the relevant chapters.

Selling

A dreary point, perhaps, but an important one nevertheless, is the problems associated with selling a property if you want to move on. There are two issues here, both of which should be considered seriously before buying a property. The first concerns repatriation of funds. In all the countries mentioned in this book there should be no problem repatriating the proceeds of the sale of a property, provided the original sum for the purchase emanated from outside the country and was brought in through the correct banking channels. Nor, in most countries, should there be a problem repatriating a reasonable profit made on the sale.

There are, however, a couple of exceptions. In Cyprus, any profit made has to be placed in a blocked account in a commercial bank on the island; the profit can only be repatriated at the rate of C£5,000 (plus interest accrued) per annum. In Turkey, any profit made is held in the Central Bank of Turkey and can only be used within the country. This might reasonably deter any potential buyers who require ready access to their assets.

The second, and more important point concerns the saleability of an apartment or villa. Some individuals have come up against difficulties trying to sell properties abroad, mainly because of competition from well-organized developers and agents. This is particularly true in areas where brand-new properties continue to be released on to the market.

A puzzle solved.

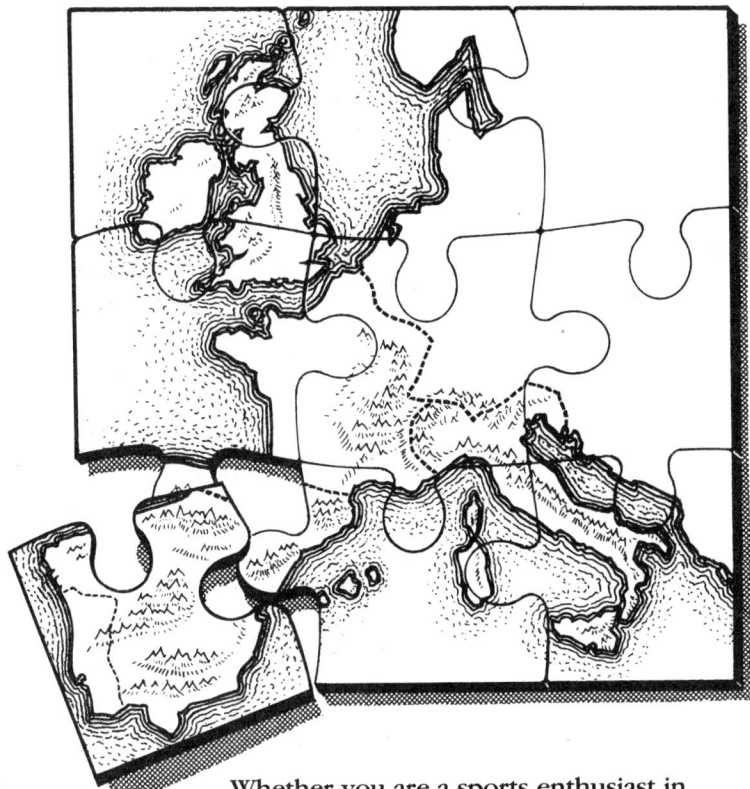

Whether you are a sports enthusiast in search of the sun, or simply in pursuit of an idyllic retreat in one of Europe's many cultural havens, we will guide you to the right solution through our own and associate offices in *Spain, Portugal, France* and *Italy.*

The European property experts.

PRIME FORCE IN PROPERTY

6 Arlington Street, St James's, London SW1A 1RB
Tel: 01-493 8222   Fax: 01-493 4921

The answer, of course, is to select a property that not only suits your tastes and needs, but that has general appeal as well. The quality of construction and interiors is important, but more important still is location. An apartment on the beach or on a golf course is far more likely to sell quickly, and more profitably, than one tucked away in a back street; similarly a ski chalet next to the lifts will sell better than one a half-hour drive from the slopes. Location, location, location: the old rule applies.

NB: The prices and legal information detailed in this book were correct at the time of writing, but should be taken as a guide only.

CHAPTER 1
FRANCE

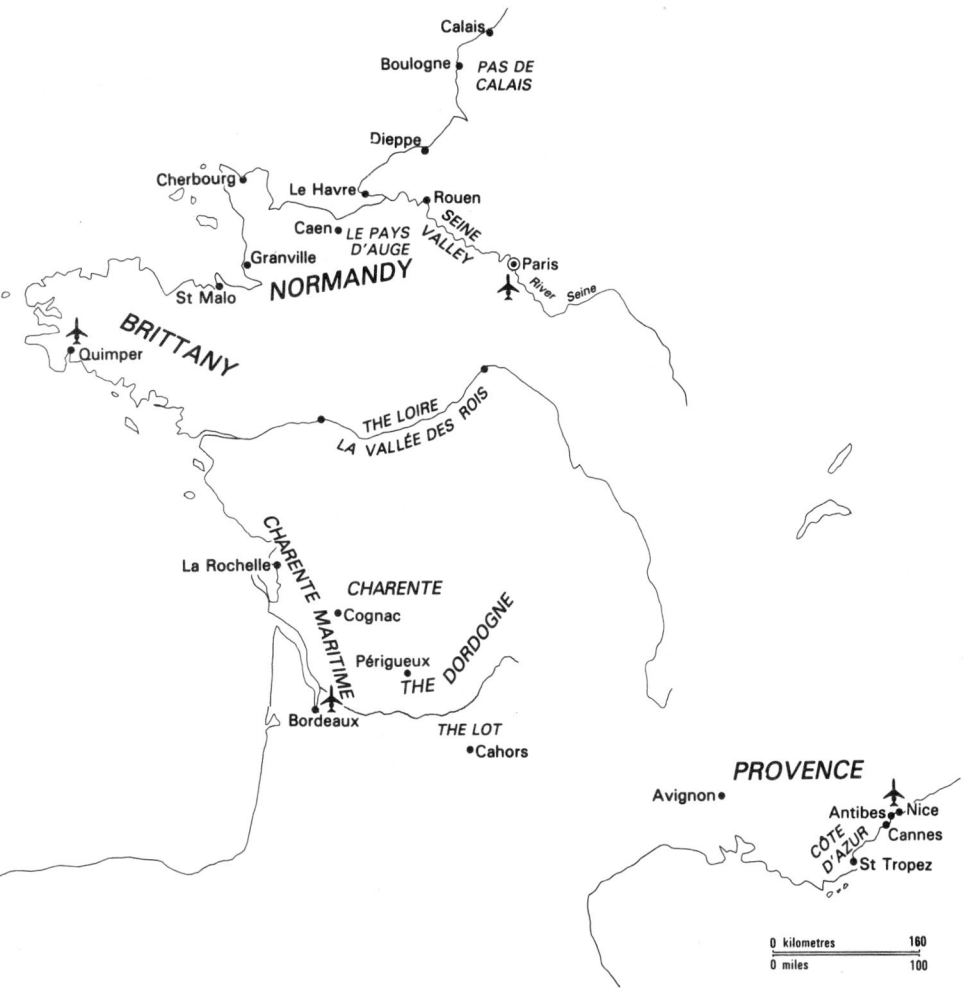

The French have always known something that the British have been reluctant to admit – that France has everything civilized man could ask for: good food, fine wines, sunshine and some of the most magnificent and varied landscape in the world. The British might still be slow to admit this, but there are, nevertheless, signs afoot that a growing number are crossing the water to buy a stake in this beautiful country. In 1988 agents selling property in France reported a fivefold increase in enquiries over the previous year.

One reason for this burst of enthusiasm might be a genuine and growing appreciation of the French quality of life; another might be the promise of easier accessibility once the Channel Tunnel is built in 1993. Yet another might be just a hint of speculation that 'smart money' is being invested in French property. Certainly the French property market is showing signs of recovery following a long, sluggish period in the early 1980s under President Mitterrand's socialist government, but it should be remembered that France is a big country – two and a half times the size of Britain – with virtually the same population. Its size is one of its beauties. Unlike Britain, with its expanding commuter belt eating into almost every corner of the little remaining countryside, France still has vast unspoilt rural expanses.

To what extent the 'British effect' will influence the property market in France has yet to be seen, bearing in mind that the French and the British have very different requirements from a home. The French want comfort, something ready to move into, and are building *pavillons*, or housing estates, to suit their needs. The British, on the other hand, often seek something a little run down that can be tinkered with, or virtually rebuilt, at leisure. In many rural areas of France there is still a stock of derelict barns, cottages and old farmhouses waiting to be restored.

One area where the British have increasingly been practising their DIY is the Pas de Calais, closer geographically to London than to Paris, and, with the opening of the Channel Tunnel, only 100 minutes on the train from Victoria.

Pas de Calais

Two years ago, few people would have contemplated buying a holiday home in the Pas de Calais. Encompassing the Channel ports Boulogne and Calais, it was the region to race through at high speed en route to warmer climes in the south. Today, however, you will be lucky to find a single farm cottage, or *fermette*, that hasn't already been snapped up by eager southerners in anticipation of the opening of the Channel Tunnel.

On the great day the 'Chunnel' will emerge from the darkness at Fréthun, just outside Calais. But few would put accessibility so high on their priority list that they would buy a property in Calais itself: it's a charmless industrial sprawl. The hinterland of Boulogne, however, is rustic and remarkably unspoiled and only half an hour's drive away. Resolutely ignored by tourists, the countryside inland is gentle and rolling in parts, rather like a bit of Kent beyond the Channel. The weather is much the same too, although the food is most definitely not. The area is renowned for some of the best restaurants in northern France: fresh river and sea fish, especially herring, as well as pâtés, charcuterie, strong cheeses and substantial stews are specialities of the region.

In this region a small, two-bedroomed *fermette*, if you're lucky enough to find one, can be bought for around £25,000. For this you might get half an acre of land thrown in, but should be prepared to pay another £10,000 or so on redecorating and fitting a modern kitchen and bath. A smaller property with, say, three main rooms and a loft, in need of substantial restoration, could be picked up for as little as £19,000–20,000. A more substantial country property with, say, three or four bedrooms, outbuildings and an acre of land might cost between £50,000 and £60,000, while in Boulogne itself, small terraced cottages can be picked up at prices long since forgotten by home buyers in the British Isles. A small townhouse with living room, kitchen and bathroom, two bedrooms and a third in the loft – admittedly in need of a lick of paint but with all services intact – recently sold for £15,000.

Pas de Calais

2–3 bed townhouse	£20,000–35,000
2 bed *fermette*	£30,000–50,000
3 bed *fermette*	£40,000–70,000
4–5 bed country house	£55,000–110,000
6–7 bed country house + cottage	£100,000–200,000

Normandy

The very essence of this conservative, rural region of France – to the French, at least – is its produce. This is the land of butter and cream, famous cheeses, cider (note, no wine is produced in the region) and that fiery and delicious apple brandy, Calvados. For the English, this northern corner of France has always held enormous appeal, more perhaps for its countryside: its lush, green valleys, its grazing herds of dappled cattle, its apple trees and wooded hills, so reminiscent of home. Indeed, this is where Roman Polanski, refused entry into England, filmed *Tess* in what was supposedly Thomas Hardy's Wessex countryside. He would have had to be careful, though, not to pan a shot of the local architecture, because besides the great cathedrals of Rouen, Coutances, Bayeux and Evreux, Normandy is an area rich in very distinctive manor houses and châteaux.

Seine valley
For weekend trips, the Seine valley is easily accessible, being within two or three hours' drive from Boulogne or Calais. Alternatively, you can sail direct to Dieppe or Le Havre. The two main towns on the River Seine, Le Havre, which takes up half the river's estuary, and Rouen, virtually rebuilt following destruction in the Second World War, are such vast industrial conglomerates that it would seem unlikely that the surrounding

countryside had much to offer. It is, however, surprisingly lovely. Just outside Le Havre is the Parc Naturel Régional de Bretonne, with Camargue horses and Scottish Highland cattle grazing in the Vernier marshes, while upstream, either side of the great loops of the Seine, the scenery is soft and lush with magnificent woods of beech and fir. A short drive takes you to the Côte Fleurie resorts of Trouville and Honfleur and the famous racing town of Deauville.

An active, wealthy area in its own right, with many country houses being owned by commuters to Rouen, Le Havre and even Caen, it is also popular with Parisians for weekend homes. Typically the properties are half-timbered; the farmhouses tend to be low-lying, often a single storey high. Alternatively, there are *maisons bourgeoises*, rather grand, classically proportioned mansions. Many come with an acre or two of land.

Seine valley

2 bed cottage	£40,000–50,000
3 bed cottage	£50,000–60,000
4–5 bed *maison bourgeoise*	£70,000–100,000

Le Pays d'Auge

The prettiest, most rustic province in Normandy, Le Pays d'Auge is an enchanting pocket of rolling green meadows, twisting country lanes, apple blossom and dairy farms, extending inland from the Côte Fleurie to the department of Orne along the Touques and Vie rivers. In Le Pays d'Auge, every town has a name more familiar on the cheese board. Camembert, for instance, the most famous of all Normandy cheeses, Livarot, Vimoutiers and Pont L'Evêque are all names derived from their towns of origin in this region. Although, sadly, few cheeses are still made in the traditional way, cider, the other great product of the area, most certainly is. Seemingly every farm gate has a signboard inviting passers-by to try a little of its very special *cidre bouché*.

The delights of the country lanes and the medieval half-timbered towns of this region are easily reached via the ports of Le Havre and Ouistreham (Caen); also via Dieppe and Cherbourg. Plans to build a new bridge from Le Havre to Honfleur in 1992 should further ease the journey, as, of course, will the Channel Tunnel and planned autoroute from Calais to Tours via Rouen.

The region is renowned for its old farmhouses and manors in crisscross soft red stonework, as pretty as the orchards in blossom; also small *calombages*, half-timbered cottages in varying states of repair, that are ideal for rustic weekend retreats. A small two-roomed cottage, for instance, about eight miles from Argentan, in need of tidying up but with water and electricity connected, recently sold for £15,000. A village house with sitting room, kitchen, bathroom and bedroom downstairs, and room for three further bedrooms upstairs, sold for £42,000; and a fully restored country house with three bedrooms and a couple of acres of land would cost £60,000.

Le Pays d'Auge

2 bed cottage	£30,000–45,000
3 bed cottage	£40,000–60,000
4–5 bed farmhouse	£70,000–100,000

Cherbourg peninsula

The Manche region, or the Cherbourg peninsula as it is better known, offers some reasonably priced country properties that are almost too good to resist. The reason is simple: the autoroute peters out at Caen, making it just too far for the Parisian weekender. Manche is, in fact, better serviced for the British than the French, with regular ferry services from Portsmouth to Cherbourg and St Malo.

The peninsula has a character and atmosphere quite different from the

CHATEAUX, COTTAGES & CALVADOS...

One of the many properties available in this special part of France.

Since establishing our connection with Normandy in 1980, we have built up an impressive portfolio of properties in this magical and accessible area of France, ranging from pretty cottages to substantial chateaux, ideal for weekends, holidays or as more permanent homes.

MAKE THE FRENCH CONNECTION
01-731 4391

rest of Normandy. Travel west from Cherbourg to La Hague, the northern tip of the peninsula, and you will find isolated, bracken-covered hills and dramatic rugged cliffs which the locals claim to be the highest in Europe. Stark, wild coastal scenes alternate with fine sandy beaches – uncrowded even in summer – and fishing villages with bobbing boats and lobster pots piled high on the quays. At the base of the peninsula is, of course, the immense sweep of the Bay of Mont St Michel, where at low tide the sea is lost from view, while inland narrow, tangled country lanes lead to the gentlest, most delightful villages and valleys.

The properties on this western stretch, unlike other parts of Normandy, tend to be built of solid local stone. As an example of the amount of property you can get for your money, an attractive stone-built house with three rooms downstairs, an attic above suitable for conversion, plus two detached outbuildings, again suitable for conversion, and half an acre of land can be bought for around £18,000. Near the ancient sea port of Granville, just north of Mont St Michel, a small château, admittedly in need of complete restoration, recently sold for £32,000. A beautifully restored six-bedroomed country house with stables and an acre of land sold for £73,000.

The Cherbourg peninsula

2 bed cottage	£25,000–40,000
3 bed cottage	£35,000–45,000
4–5 bed country house	£50,000–70,000
6–7 bed country house	£70,000–100,000

Brittany

After the Côte d'Azur, Brittany is the most popular resort area in France, for one very obvious reason: the sea. A low-lying peninsula pushing west from the Channel into the Atlantic Ocean, Brittany has over 900 miles of tortuously indented and beautiful coastline: wild and ruddy-coloured rocky headlands, interspersed with gracious inlets and gentle beaches of fine white sand, sometimes narrow, sometimes stretching as far as the eye can see. There are offshore islands and islets too, and everywhere the stone dolmens and menhir monuments of a prehistoric past.

History is something that cannot be ignored in this land of tough and resilient people, still touched by their Celtic culture. West of a line from St Brieuc to Vannes, the locals can occasionally be heard to speak Breton (as well as French, of course), derived from the Celtic refugees who fled from the Anglo-Saxon invasions and gave the province its name and its character. The dwellings – small, sturdy stone cottages – are remarkably like those found in Cornwall or the Welsh hills, as are the small, peaceful fishing communities built around a row of simple waterfront cottages.

Nowhere are these more evident than in the western *département* of Finistère, the Land's End of Brittany.

In Finistère, and along the southern coast – superb for sailing, fishing and water sports of all descriptions – some of the best property buys can be found. Proximity to the beach naturally pushes prices up, but inland, in the peaceful rolling countryside, stone cottages can be found at remarkably low prices. About the cheapest on the market recently was a tiny run-down stone cottage with two rooms and a loft, ten miles from the beach, price £8,000. An old millhouse, shabby but habitable, with two bedrooms, outbuildings and a good chunk of land, cost £37,000. For the less adventurous, a fully modernized three-bedroomed house near the coast might cost between £40,000 and £50,000.

Flights to the region can be made direct from Gatwick to Finistère's ancient capital, Quimper. Alternatively ferries run from Portsmouth to St Malo, about two hours' drive to the north.

Brittany

2 bed cottage	£30,000–45,000
3 bed cottage	£40,000–60,000
4–5 bed house	£70,000–90,000

The Loire

The longest and one of the finest rivers in France, the Loire flows north from its source in the Massif Central, then west towards the Atlantic along the broad, prosperous and densely populated valley aptly named La Vallée des Rois, the Valley of the Kings. More than the Loire itself – at this point wide and shallow, full of islands and whirling currents – it is the fairytale Renaissance châteaux, seemingly hundreds of them, dotted regally along the river between Orléans in the east and Nantes in the west, that faithfully draw in the crowds.

It is the châteaux – Chenonceaux, Azay-le-Rideau and Loches among the finest – as well as the riverside towns and villages that give the Loire valley its character, although parts of it, it has to be said, are far from picturesque. With prosperity, needless to say, comes industry. Some of the prettiest spots are not along the Loire itself, but along its tributaries: the Cher, Vienne and Indre. Here the river banks are also more accessible for picnics of cheese and fruit and delicate white Loire wines.

Within an easy day's drive of the Channel ports, the properties affordable for holiday homes in the Loire share one thing in common with their rather grander counterparts. Château or cottage, properties in the Loire are typically constructed of local tufa stone, a pale stone that has the curious quality of turning even paler as time passes by. All types of properties are available from *fermettes* to small village houses, villas and townhouses, even small châteaux, some fully modernized and others in a state of disrepair. Rock-bottom price would be around £15,000 for a run-down *fermette* in need of renovation, perhaps with a barn and half an acre of land. Moving up the scale, you could buy an attractive three-bedroomed house ready to move into, in the country or in a village, for around £40,000. A smart four-bedroomed villa could cost around £65,000.

The Loire

2 bed *fermette*	£30,000–40,000
3 bed house	£40,000–60,000
4 bed house	£60,000–80,000
small château	£100,000–250,000

The Dordogne

'Just to glimpse the mysterious river Dordogne is something to be grateful for all one's life . . . it is the nearest thing to Paradise this side of Greece.' So wrote Henry Miller, echoing the sentiments of many travellers who have laid eyes on this most beautiful of rivers meandering lavishly and gently through the heart of the region.

The Dordogne in south-west France, lush and picturesque, with abrupt escarpments and hills, often topped with ancient castles rising from gentle meadows and river valleys, has long been favoured by the British seeking a taste of French rural life and of its world-famous cuisine: pâté de foie gras, wild *cèpes* and, of course, that other curious wild fungus, the truffle. The central part of the Dordogne, divided into Périgord Blanc, named after its pale chalky soil, and Périgord Noir, where oak trees hug the banks of the River Dordogne, are the most popular regions of all. Further north and east, beyond Brive and Limoges, the hills become steeper and the valleys deeper as one climbs to the river's source in the Massif Central.

The region is also rich in examples of the most ancient art form of all: the prehistoric cave paintings of animals at Les Eysies and Pech-Merle, shaped to the form of the rock, and signed in the only way the artist knew how, with a handprint. These wonderful and awesome sights are within eight or nine hours' drive of the Channel ports.

The Dordogne has numerous little hamlets providing an abundance of delightful rural properties, but alas, the English discovered the heart of the region, in Pèrigord, long ago and the stock of bargain properties in need of renovation is running dry. Five years ago you could buy a run-down farmhouse for around £15,000. A similar property today costs double that, although derelict properties needing renovation can still be picked up for around £20,000 if you venture away from the central region, north of Périgueux. Restored properties, typically with steeply pitched roofs curving gently as a ski jump towards the eaves, can, of course, be bought in the north or south of the Dordogne. Périgord Noir also boasts some of the most beautiful châteaux in south-west France. Overlooking the River Vezère, for example, an immaculate sixteenth-century château, complete with studded oak doors and salon lined with silk, was recently on offer for £570,000.

The Dordogne

2 bed village house, without garden	£30,000–40,000
2 bed country cottage	£35,000–45,000
3 bed *fermette*	£50,000–70,000
4–5 bed country house + outbuildings	£80,000–130,000
château + 10–20 acres	£250,000–600,000

Charente

A low-lying, undramatic land to the west of the Dordogne, Charente remains somehow undiscovered. Simple, unpretentious and totally unspoilt, it's a region of gentle hills, wide rivers, vast pine forests and, most beautiful of all, exquisite Romanesque churches dotted, as if for ever there, across the countryside. It is also the land of cognac.

Cognac the town lies in the peaceful fertile valley of the River Charente, surrounded by vine-covered hills stretching as far as the eye can see. The name is not all that gives the town's activities away. The smell of fermenting brandy is everywhere, as you step off the train or out of your car, in the crooked medieval lanes by the river, and, naturally enough, around the warehouses and great distilleries that dominate the town. The walls of buildings – inside and out – are streaked black by a tiny fungus that thrives on the fumes of the precious, intoxicating liquid that are lost into the atmosphere – the angels' share, as the distillers call it. Outside the town the cognac producers' share is apparent in the form of small châteaux rising elegantly above the wooded slopes.

The farmhouses in the Charente valley are low-lying and ochre-coloured, with shallow-pitched roofs reflecting the dry, warm microclimate of this westerly pocket of France. Generally there is a greater supply of reasonably priced properties still in need of renovation than in Charente's neighbour, the Dordogne. It is still possible, for instance, to pick up a derelict nineteenth-century *fermette* for under £20,000, often with an adjoining sandy-coloured barn built as a continuation of the house itself. A run-down village house in Aujac, 15 miles north of Cognac, was recently on the market for just £13,000. In the Charente valley towards Saintes, a three-bedroomed *ferme Charentaise*, fully restored, with additional outbuildings suitable for conversion, sold for

£53,000. The region is about a six-hour drive from the Channel ports, being easily accessible from the main Tour–Poitiers autoroute. Alternatively you can fly to Bordeaux, about an hour's drive to the south.

Charente

2 bed village house	£15,000–25,000
3 bed village house	£25,000–40,000
3 bed country house	£40,000–55,000
4–5 bed country house	£50,000–70,000

Charente Maritime

Not as chic as the Côte d'Azur, Charente Maritime nevertheless enjoys almost as many sunshine hours and is within a comfortable day's drive of the UK. It's distinctly Atlantic in character, with dunes, pine forests, extensive marshland and long, ocean-washed sandy beaches – not the cleanest in the world, but with shallow waters suitable for families with young children. Dotted along the coastline, the islands of Ré, Oléron and Noirmoutier have an unsophisticated charm of their own, while La Rochelle, one of the country's longest-established ports, is also one of the prettiest and most distinctive resorts in France.

On the coast itself there are very few properties of any character; most are small apartment blocks favoured by Parisian *Mamas et les enfants* visiting for the summer months. It's a convenient spot for them, close enough to Paris for *Papa* to join them at the weekends. A little inland, however, in gentle rolling countryside – still within a couple of miles of the beach – there is an ample supply of country and village properties, some needing work and others fully restored. Generally they are more reasonably priced north of La Rochelle, towards La Roche and Partheney.

Charente Maritime
(within a few miles of the beach)

2 bed village house	£25,000–35,000
3 bed village house	£35,000–40,000
3 bed country house	£50,000–65,000
4–5 bed country house	£60,000–80,000

The Lot

Travelling south and east of the Dordogne, you leave behind the lush, verdant countryside of its river valleys in place of a more barren, parched landscape, characteristic of the region of the River Lot. Here you begin to feel the intensity of the Mediterranean sun. The houses are white, built of traditional *quercy blanc* stone, the older ones featuring distinctive square pigeon towers and wooden balconies adorned with climbing vines. Perched on hilltops are ancient villages and fortified towns acting as a reminder of the Hundred Years' War, their medieval houses clustered around a solid church or perhaps a château in streets so narrow that neighbours can shake hands by leaning across from their balconies. At the centre of the region is the historic town of Cahors, famous for its full-blooded red wines.

Much of the countryside in the Lot remains undiscovered by summer visitors. Far enough inland to enjoy a quiet pastoral way of life, it is still possible here to find a cheap, run-down *fermette* for as little as £10,000. It's possible, too, to pick up a sizeable property and good acreage for your money. As an example, a substantial stone house for modernization about ten miles from Cahors recently came on the market at £37,000; this included a second house and extensive outbuildings. A remote but fully restored farmhouse with three bedrooms, outbuildings, a small two-roomed cottage and 20 acres of land sold for £73,000.

The Lot

2 bed village house	£30,000–40,000
3 bed country house	£40,000–70,000
4–5 bed country house + 10 acres	£60,000-120,000

Provence

Ruled and divided between Greeks and Romans, Saracens, popes and foreign dukes, Provence has the most ancient of all civilizations in France. The Romans ruled it as a province of Rome – hence the name, and hence, too, the baths at Aix, the theatre at Orange and the amphitheatre at Arles, some of the most perfect monuments of the classical world. In more recent times, the great impressionists – Gauguin, Renoir, Van Gogh and Cézanne – chose Provence not so much for its historical sites as for the vitality of its landscape, the clarity of its light and the brilliance of its colours. Today Provence continues to captivate the visitor with its warm open-air life, its terraced hills and woods of cork and sweet-smelling pine, its *citadelles* perched high on rocky escarpments and its old men drinking pastis and playing boules in village squares; also, its proximity to the Mediterranean coast and the ski slopes of St Etienne;

and, not least of all, its Provençal cuisine seasoned with garlic, basil and thyme.

Sadly it is no longer possible to find the inexpensive farmhouses with an acre or two of land that one can still track down in south-western France. The cheapest property you could hope for would be a *bergerie*, or sheep pen, for around £40,000. Although this may sound affordable, all you are in fact buying is a plot of land, a beautiful view and permission to build. The idea, of course, would be to convert the original building, but it might be cheaper to knock it down and start again. A restored farmhouse, away from the coast with, say, three bedrooms might cost around £100,000. Recently a fourteenth-century four-bedroomed farmhouse near Vaison la Romaine, about half an hour's drive north of Avignon, sold for £173,000; the price included around 25 acres of land. In the southern Var region, property is more expensive the closer it is to the Côte d'Azur.

Provence

2 bed village house	£40,000–60,000
3 bed village house	£50,000–80,000
3 bed country house	£60,000–100,000
4 bed country house	£90,000–180,000
5 bed country house	£130,000–250,000

Côte d'Azur

Over-populated, over-developed and in the summer months unbearably over-congested with traffic, the Côte d'Azur – stretching from Cannes to the Italian border, and taking in Nice and Antibes – has little to do with France. It is an international resort with international prices, one of the most expensive stretches of coastline in the world.

It was discovered by the British in 1834 when Lord Brougham, *en route* to Italy, was forced to stay briefly in Cannes and remained just long enough to buy a small plot of land. Cannes was no more than a fishing village then, but, protected from the northern winds by the Alps and the Esterel mountains, it enjoyed a wonderful year-round climate. Lord Brougham built a villa and was soon followed by his friends; and so the Côte d'Azur was put on the map of international resorts.

A hundred and fifty years on, the wealthy parade in million-dollar yachts and spend lavishly in the numerous restaurants and casinos; the glorious villas of yesteryear, in secret gardens of mimosa and bougainvillea, have been replaced with apartment blocks more suited to modern standards of comfort and manageability. None the less, the natural beauty of this remarkable coastline – its hills and islands and warm, aromatic Mediterranean vegetation – remains. It would be difficult even for man to destroy it.

Property, as with living, is expensive in the south of France, but the joy is that its continued popularity ensures good returns both from letting and resale at the end of the day. Few can afford the millions required for a seafront villa in Cannes and Antibes, but more realistic prices are being asked for smaller properties in modern developments, near to but not quite in the centre of town. At Cannes Marina, for example – not in fact in Cannes, but built around a lagoon ten minutes' drive away – studio apartments are selling from £47,000; while at the other end of the scale a three-bedroomed penthouse costs £215,000. Lying back and above the Route de Nice just outside Antibes, studio apartments in a small development with communal gardens and pool start at £40,000. Prices vary enormously depending on quality and, most of all, location. In Nice, for example, a smart three-bedroomed apartment with small private garden and perhaps a tiny pool can cost upwards of £400,000.

Côte d'Azur

Studio apartment	£35,000–65,000
1 bed apartment	£70,000–100,000
2 bed apartment	£100,000–200,000
3 bed apartment	£150,000–350,000

If all that is required is a holiday pad, small and compact and easy to run, one option is to buy an apartment on sale-and-leaseback. Under this scheme you can buy a property at a reduced price – usually a 30 per cent reduction – in return for surrendering the rental rights for a specified period of time, usually eleven years, during which you retain use of the property for a given number of weeks a year (see pages 129–130). At Cap Esterel, for instance, a complete self-contained resort covering 580 acres on the coast between Agay and St Raphael, fully furnished studio flats are selling on sale-and-leaseback for £36,000. A one-bedder costs £52,500. For this you get six weeks' use of the apartment a year plus full use of the shared amenities: cafés, restaurants, swimming pools, tennis courts, private beach and private golf course, winding and undulating its way around the village. A similar scheme is on offer at Mont d'Azur, a development set high up in the hills between Valbonne and the fortified village of Biot. Commanding spectacular views of the Riviera from Cannes to the snow-capped mountains of the Alpes Maritimes, a four-bedroomed villa with half an acre and swimming pool costs from £250,000.

But perhaps of all the developments on the Côte d'Azur the one that takes the biscuit is Port Grimaud, a little Venice in the Gulf of St Tropez. Designed by architect François Spoerry, Port Grimaud has gained worldwide recognition as the most successful and skilfully designed marina project of its kind. It has been built as a complete village with shops, cafés, a market twice a week, post office, tennis club, even a

FRANCE

Since 1972 we have specialised in selling properties exclusively throughout France and in providing a full advisory service on all aspects of property purchase.

We have property lists from many regions including PAS DE CALAIS - NORMANDY - LOIRE - CHARENTES - DORDOGNE - LOT - ARDECHE - TARN and GARONNE - LANGUEDOC - PROVENCE. Properties include barns and cottages in delightful rural surroundings from about £10,000, to Chateaux and villas.

For details of our services and our free booklet on property purchase in France, contact MICHAEL FARRANT.

Estd. 1972

FRENCH ASSOCIATES
ROBERTSBRIDGE HOUSE
ROBERTSBRIDGE, SUSSEX TN32 5AN
Tel: (0580) 880599

cinema and a church – all on a network of waterways. Two-bedroomed apartments, all built in traditional Provençal style with local tiles and other materials, cost from £136,000; a studio apartment costs from £50,000. Although no more than twenty years old, Port Grimaud has become as much a part of the environment as the ancient Provencal villages perched high on the hilltops.

Buying

Purchasing property in France is relatively straightforward. One advantage it offers over the English system is that there is no equivalent of 'subject to contract'. Consequently there is little fear of being gazumped. Once you have found a property you want, you sign a preliminary agreement, pay a deposit, and that is that. There is no turning back.

Legal charges, however, may seem a bit steep. Whereas in Britain it is customary for the vendor and purchaser each to be represented by his own lawyer, in France there is only one notary public (*notaire*) who represents both parties. You should insist on using your own choice of *notaire*, preferably one who speaks English. After all, you as the purchaser will be paying his fee, which is usually around 2½ per cent of the purchase price of the property. On top of this, there is a registration tax (similar to our stamp duty) of 8–9 per cent on properties over five years old.

Having found a property you want to buy, the first thing you will be asked to do is to sign a preliminary contract (*compromis de vente*) and pay a deposit of 10 per cent. The deposit is paid to the *notaire*, never to the vendor. From this point you are committed, unless by any chance you fail to obtain a loan, or, in the case of older properties, the planning status of the property cannot be confirmed. If you are unlucky enough to deal with a vendor who pulls out, you are entitled to your deposit back, plus an equal sum in compensation.

Completion of the document usually takes between sixty and ninety days. During this period the *notaire* will prepare the conveyance document (*acte*), a draft of which must be vetted by both you and a qualified professional. On signing the *acte*, title of the property changes hands. You hand over the money and the property is yours.

Signing the *acte* must take place in the *notaire*'s office, and if you cannot attend – a common event in the case of British purchasers – power of attorney can be granted to someone else on your behalf.

Finally, the *acte* will be sent by the *notaire* to the land registry for official registration. It may be a couple of months before the document can be collected, but possession of the document in itself is not proof of ownership. This is provided by the land registry and guaranteed by the state.

In the case of new properties, the procedure is somewhat different, especially if the building is not yet completed. You will be asked to sign a preliminary agreement as before, but the deposit will be much less – usually between 2½ and 5 per cent. Stage payments will then be made as construction proceeds. It is the law in France that all new developments must be underwritten by a bank. Check that your developer has this cover so that you will be protected in the event of failure to deliver.

Selling

If and when you come to sell a property in France, it is likely that it will be worth more than when you bought it. If this is the case, and the property is not your principal residence, then you will be subject to capital gains tax at 33 per cent. However, there are several allowances that can reduce this tax liability considerably.

The most important allowance to be aware of, right from the time of purchase, is on the cost of home improvements. Improvement costs are tax-deductible provided you can supply receipted invoices issued by the builders. 'Back-of-an-envelope' receipts will not be accepted. If you happen to be a DIY fanatic, remember to keep the receipts for building materials. The value of these will be multiplied by three to compensate you for your labour.

Other deductible expenses include legal charges, agency commission and a generous allowance to account for inflation. If you keep a property for twenty-two years or more you will not be subject to capital gains tax at all.

As for getting your money out of France on resale of a property, there is no problem provided that the property was originally paid for with funds emanating from outside France and that this fact was recorded in the purchase deed.

CHAPTER 2
ITALY

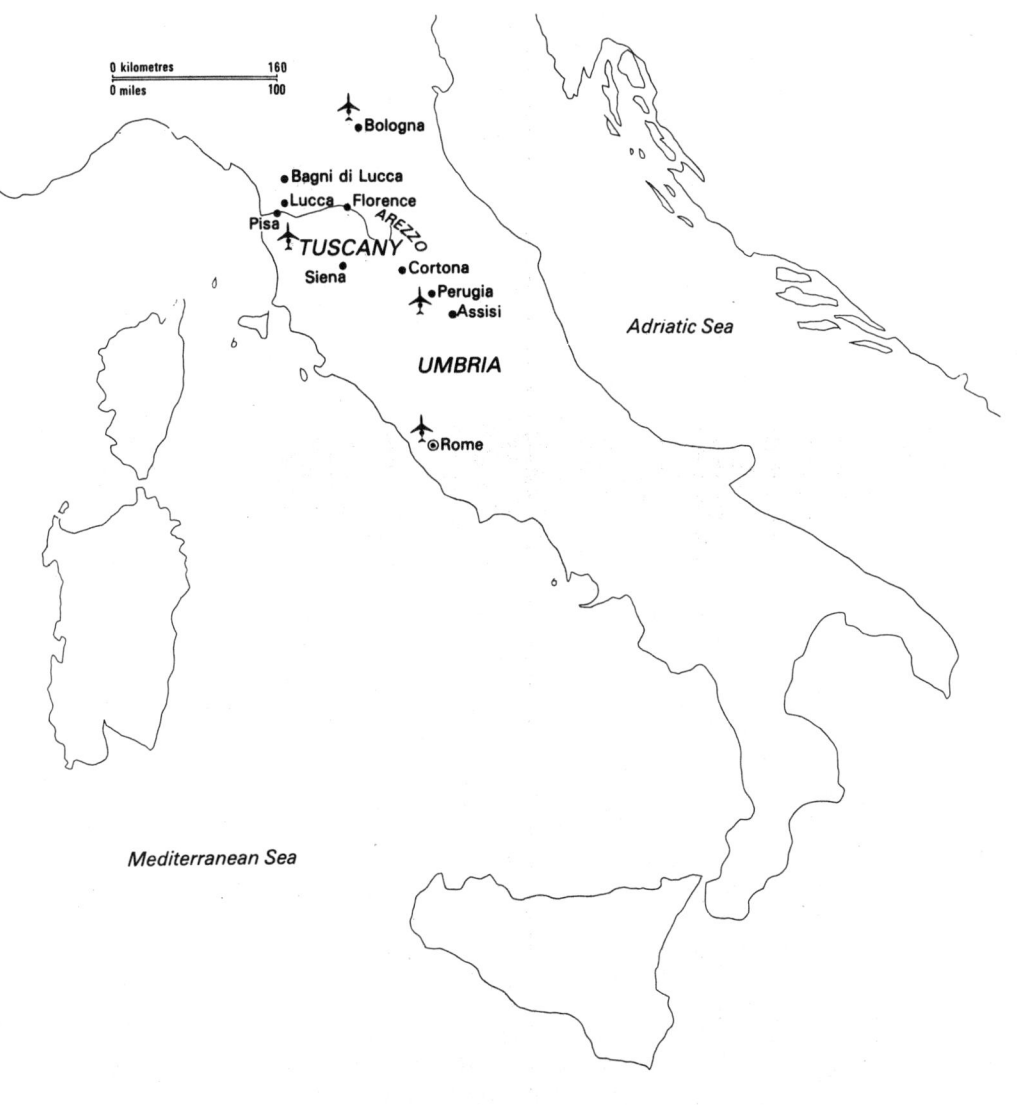

Italy may not be renowned for beaches and package tours, but it has always had its devotees among those who put culture and food before sea and sand. Since early Victorian times the English have visited Italy, and in particular Tuscany, for its ancient civilization and Renaissance art.

Strangely enough, though, the market for property in Italy is relatively small – at least for foreigners. In contrast to Spain and Portugal, for instance, you do not see columns of Italian properties for sale in the Sunday papers, although the Italians themselves put great store in bricks and mortar. Internally, the market is buoyant as the locals buy up property as a secure investment, and as a result capital appreciation is one of the highest in Europe. On average, property prices in Italy have been rising by 10–15 per cent a year, and in some areas by as much as 30 per cent a year. The absence of developments geared specifically at the foreign investor, however, means that there is no easy way to buy into the Italian property market. Would-be buyers, armed with lists produced by just a handful of British agents, must take to the hills and do their own prospecting among rural properties.

Tuscany

No one could fail to be seduced by the cultural and historical magnificence that Tuscany has to offer. It was the centre of the Renaissance, and before that of Etruscan and Roman culture; and today its historic towns – Florence, Siena, Lucca and Pisa – still burst with art and music and all things lovely. In the surrounding hills, ancient villages and Tuscan farmhouses nestle peacefully among the vineyards and terraced olive groves.

If there is one region in Italy where Britons have bought property, this is it. Indeed, it is often referred to as a little Gloucestershire in rural Italy. However, the stock of ancient stone dwellings has not dried up completely. Away from tarmac roads, empty farmhouses, abandoned long ago by subsistence farmers, can still be found dotted across the countryside. The price and availability of properties still to be restored varies enormously from one region of Tuscany to another, but generally property is more expensive the closer it is to Florence.

Florence to Siena
At the heart of Tuscany lie the green hills of the famous wine-producing area of Chianti. Walled medieval villages, turreted hilltop villas, tall cypress trees, umbrella pines and terraced slopes of vineyards dominate the landscape. It is everyone's vision of Tuscany. Florence, with its fine churches and magnificent collection of art, lies to the north; the ancient town of Siena, perched on three hilltops, to the south. To the west, situated on the heights of a splendid hill, stands the village of San Gimignano, dominated by its medieval towers. Pisa and Bologna airports

are both within an hour and a half's drive, and Rome is just two hours' drive to the south.

Although readily accessible, the countryside south and west of Florence has remained largely unspoilt due to strict planning controls. No amount of protection, however, could possibly have controlled the escalation of property prices in the region. Its popularity has pushed it to the top of the price league in rural Italy; £40,000 would be considered rock-bottom for a small country cottage in this region – even unrestored.

Take, for example, a derelict house and cottage with barn attached between San Gimignano and Volterra, price £58,000; or a tumbledown millhouse with no floor dividing upstair from down and little sign of a roof, price £55,000. Admittedly, you get a couple of acres thrown in as well, but you would need a scythe to cut your way through to the front door – or entrance where a front door should be. A larger property, say with ten large rooms for restoration in the heart of Chianti country, might cost between £70,000 and £85,000. Although it is possible to get quite a sizeable property for your money, it's advisable to allow twice, even three times the purchase price for restoring a rural wreck into a comfortable home. The restoration costs will, of course, vary depending on its original state of disrepair, as well as its accessibility and whether or not there are electricity and water supplies nearby.

The alternative is to buy a property already restored. Some of the best buys can be found nestling in hilltop villages. A two-bedroomed apartment, for example, in an old medieval building, with large reception room, kitchen and bathroom, could be bought for £50,000 or £60,000. At the other end of the scale, a restored five-bedroomed farmhouse with huge open fireplaces, rustic red-tiled roof, thick stone walls and the vaulted ceilings so characteristic of the region might cost around £300,000.

Florence to Siena

1 bed village house, restored	£40,000–50,000
2 bed village house, restored	£50,000–60,000
2 bed farmhouse, restored	£100,000–125,000
3 bed farmhouse, restored	£125,000–160,000
4 bed farmhouse, restored	£160,000–210,000
5–8 bed farmhouse, restored	£250,000–500,000

Lucca

The northernmost province of Tuscany, Lucca borders Liguria to the north and east and Emilia to the north and west. It includes the fashionable Versilian Riviera resorts of Viareggio and Forte dei Marmi, as well as the ancient, historic towns of Castiglione, Castelnuovo and Garfagnana, and, of course, the walled medieval town of Lucca itself. The countryside is rich and varied, mountainous in parts, with many small lakes and rivers. It's here that the famous Carrara marble is quarried in the Apuan mountains. Strategically placed for a balanced mix of culture, sun and sport – a short drive takes you to the Apennine ski resort of Abetone – Lucca is also easily accessible. Most areas in the province are within half or three-quarters of an hour's drive of Pisa airport.

Although not as expensive as Chianti, the area immediately surrounding the town of Lucca is no longer cheap. At the top end of the market, for instance, a magnificent five-bedroomed eighteenth-century villa on the outskirts recently sold for £690,000. A substantial and well-restored farmhouse offering four bedrooms on the edge of a charming medieval village close to Lucca sold for £220,000; while a modernized six-bedroomed villa made £235,000.

It is possible, however, to pick up more reasonable properties a little further away. An attractive eighteenth-century farmhouse in basic habitable condition, with water and electricity, might cost around £60,000. A small two-bedroomed village house could be picked up for £40,000. A similar property in need of complete restoration could cost as little as £20,000–25,000.

Lucca

1 bed village house, restored	£30,000–40,000
2 bed village house, restored	£40,000–50,000
2 bed farmhouse, restored	£75,000–100,000
3 bed farmhouse, restored	£85,000–135,000
4 bed farmhouse, restored	£125,000–180,000
5–8 bed farmhouse, restored	£200,000–400,000

Bagni di Lucca

Still within the province of Lucca, Bagni di Lucca is a small spa town some 15 miles north of the town of Lucca. A hundred years ago, this somewhat imperial town was a popular retreat for European nobility. Dukes and marquises could be counted in their dozens sitting in cafés awaiting an evening's entertainment at the Teatro Academico or the neo-classical casino, the first gambling house in Europe. It was the British discovering the therapeutic qualities of its waters that first put the town on the social map of Europe; the surrounding hills and river valleys were quickly christened the 'Switzerland of Tuscany'. Today, Bagni di Lucca has faded into obscurity, but the thermal waters still spring from the slopes of the Corsena Hills and the scenery is still as beautiful.

It is about a two-hour drive from Pisa, so it is essential to have a car if you are considering buying in this region. The cheapness of the properties, however, should be more than compensation. Cottages and farmhouses in the small hamlets and wooded countryside surrounding Bagni di Lucca sell for a fraction of the price of those in more established areas of Tuscany. A small run-down country cottage, for instance, can be picked up for under £10,000. Recently an old mill, admittedly in need of considerable love and tender care, was on the market for £7300. A run-down two-bedroomed cottage in a hilltop village might cost between £15,000 and £20,000. There are fewer large farmhouses in the area in need of restoration, but modernized ones can be picked up for as little as £95,000. Usually the price will include two or three acres of land.

Bagni di Lucca

2 bed country cottage, restored	£30,000–35,000
3 bed country cottage, restored	£35,000–65,000
3–4 bed farmhouse, restored	£95,000–105,000
6–10 bed farmhouse, restored	£145,000–160,000

Cortona and Arezzo

South and east of Florence in the Tuscan province of Arezzo lies the magnificent rectangular walled town of Cortona. Standing high on a hilltop, its intriguing narrow streets, its ancient palazzi and churches, its excellent restaurants and its Sunday best-dressed inhabitants strolling the streets in the early evening hours offer an unadulterated and heart-warming taste of Italian life. A walk to the ancient city gates reveals a panoramic view of the wide fertile plain of Val Chiana, stretching out to the hills of Siena and the great shining expanse of Lake Trasimene.

Only a few years ago ancient farmhouses and cottages in the villages surrounding Cortona could be picked up quite reasonably, as they still can in more remote parts of Arezzo. In the last couple of years, however, prices have shot up, almost matching those around Florence and Siena. An old manor house, for instance, in reasonable condition but in need of modernization, with ten acres of olive groves and vines, costs around £250,000. A stone farmhouse in the Cortona hills with, say, two bedrooms and an independent studio apartment, costs around £135,000. Cortona is just fifteen minutes' drive off the main Florence–Rome autostrada, equidistant from Rome and Pisa airports.

Cortona and Arezzo

1 bed village house, restored	£35,000–45,000
2 bed village house, restored	£45,000–60,000
2 bed farmhouse, restored	£90,000–115,000
3 bed farmhouse, restored	£100,000–135,000
4 bed farmhouse, restored	£135,000–190,000
5–8 bed farmhouse, restored	£230,000–450,000

Umbria

Tuscany's southerly and equally lovely neighbour is aptly named the Green Heart of Italy. The rich green canvas of its woodland and tobacco fields is broken only by the deeper hues of vineyards and olive groves.

Until recently Umbria was, some would say, blessed in being bypassed by the main autostrada from Milan, through Florence and Rome, to Reggio di Calabria in the south. It was off the beaten track – and property, in plentiful supply, was cheap.

In the last few years, however, main roads have been carved through Umbria, putting some of Europe's most beautiful towns – Assisi and Perugia, to name just two – firmly on the tourist map. Rome and Pisa airports are now within a couple of hours' drive, and there is talk of upgrading the airport at Perugia to international status. Umbria is becoming accessible, and property prices, although still considerably lower than in Tuscany, have been rising at between 25 and 30 per cent a year. Many experts speculate that property prices in the two regions will be at level pegging within three or four years.

As in Tuscany, ancient farm buildings lie scattered across the countryside, abandoned over thirty years ago by subsistence farmers who left the land for the promise of a better life in the towns. The difference in Umbria is the sheer number of tumbledown cottages, barns, tobacco-drying towers and farmhouses still standing empty, just waiting to be renovated into glorious rural retreats. Most of the farm buildings in Umbria are two or three hundred years old, and some are medieval. Compared with Tuscan farmhouses they are somewhat smaller in scale, with fewer arches and simpler lines. Nevertheless, they are full of charm and mostly enjoy magnificent views, even though some have not been lived in for decades.

Take, for example, a derelict two-bedroomed cottage, accessible only by a narrow, stony road winding up into the hills. Complete with geese and the odd chicken, the price tag is £20,000. A four-bedroomed house in a similarly dilapidated state costs between £30,000 and £40,000; a medieval house between £85,000 and £110,000. The condition of these country properties varies from merely derelict to completely ruinous with holes in the roof and no floor dividing the ground floor from what would be the upstairs.

For the less adventurous there are, of course, properties that have already been restored. A two-bedroomed apartment, for instance, forming part of a large farm building in the upper Tiber valley would cost about £34,000; a small two-bedroomed house on the edge of a village near Umbertide, £45,000. Again in the upper Tiber valley, a large farmhouse with external staircase and three bedrooms costs about £93,000.

Umbria

1 bed apartment in village or town, restored	£20,000–25,000
2 bed cottage, restored	£25,000–40,000
3–4 bed farmhouse, restored	£35,000–65,000
5–6 bed farmhouse, restored	£65,000–105,000
large villa or palazzo, restored	£160,000–350,000

Restoring

Renovating a tumbledown wreck in rural Italy is no task to be taken on lightly, particularly if you intend to carry out the work from the comfort of your armchair at home. Apart from the problem of language, there are innumerable snags concerning planning regulations, the supply of materials, building work and so on, that will inevitably arise. The most likely route to success is to employ a *geometra*. A Jack of all trades – surveying, construction, law, accountancy and estate management – he will oversee the building work for you in your absence.

While the work is being done, you might consider putting in a swimming pool. Local authorities don't usually object, providing it doesn't tap the village water supply or upset anyone's view, and it could prove a lucrative investment. A 12×4 metre pool costs between £12,000 and £15,000 to install, but in return you could push your property into the league of highly desirable residences for letting. A villa in central Tuscany sleeping ten, with pool and tennis court, can attract a high-season rental of £1500 a week. A smaller four-bedroomed house, with pool, could net a weekly income of between £800 and £1200.

Don't go overboard, though, in creating a luxurious investment property. Any renovation work must be in keeping with the traditional architecture, which means that large picture windows and smart new extensions are out of the question. Some local authorities will not even allow the conversion of the ground floor: that, they say, is meant for the animals. The Italians are protective of their heritage to the extent that even the division of plots follow the lines established in the Middle Ages. To your advantage, this means that it is virtually impossible for developers to gain planning permission to construct new developments that might possibly destroy your unspoilt view of rural Italy.

Buying

Purchasing a house in Italy rarely works out according to the book; even the simplest of transactions in this Latin country can cause complications. However, you shouldn't let this put you off. The ownership of every brick and every square metre of land in Italy is meticulously registered in the books of the local commune, and, providing the wording is correct, the purchaser is fully protected.

Having selected a property, the first step is to arrange for a survey and all the necessary searches required for legal transfer. As well as checking documentation, your solicitor should look into the ownership of the property; sometimes several members of a family may share a title. He should also check that the vendor has no outstanding taxes to pay from previous transactions. If he does, you as the buyer could become liable.

Usually a *geometra* is employed to check the boundaries of the property and generally sort out matters pertaining to the house. In the case of agricultural land, checks should be made to ensure that none of the immediate neighbours of the property in question wishes to buy it at the agreed price. If they do, they have priority on purchase – although it should be said that this very rarely occurs.

Providing all runs smoothly, the next stage is to sign a *compromesso*, or preliminary contract of sale, and pay a non-returnable deposit which is usually between 20 and 30 per cent of the agreed price. The *compromesso* is a binding contract on both parties. If you subsequently pull out, you lose your deposit, while if the vendor pulls out, he will be legally bound to pay you twice the sum of the deposit in compensation.

Between one and three months later, after the appropriate searches at the local land registry have been carried out, the transfer deed (*rogito*) is signed in the offices of the local notary. The money is handed over and the transaction completed. All that is left to do then is for the notary to register the transfer deed with the local land registry.

In the case of a new or refurbished property bought direct from a developer, the buyer is charged 6 per cent VAT. In addition, transfer costs incurred include a 2 per cent notary's fee and a registration tax payable at 10 per cent on houses and 17 per cent on land. These fees, however, are calculated not as a percentage of the full value of the property, as might be expected, but as a percentage of the commercial value of the property determined by reference to its statutory income, or *reddito catastale*, registered, specifically for this purpose, at the land registry. For an average property, the commercial value will usually be between 50 and 60 per cent of the full value of the property. This anomaly, approved by the Italian government, not only cuts down the registration tax paid by the purchaser, but also the capital gains tax, or INVIM, paid by the vendor.

Selling

If and when you sell a property in Italy, capital gains tax is paid on a sliding scale ranging from a minimum of 3 per cent to a maximum of 30 per cent, and takes into account any improvements that have been made. Around 10–11 per cent is the usual figure. Repatriation of funds is not a problem, providing the funds for purchasing the property are transferred from outside Italy through normal banking channels. It is essential that purchasing funds come from an external source.

CHAPTER 3
MAINLAND SPAIN

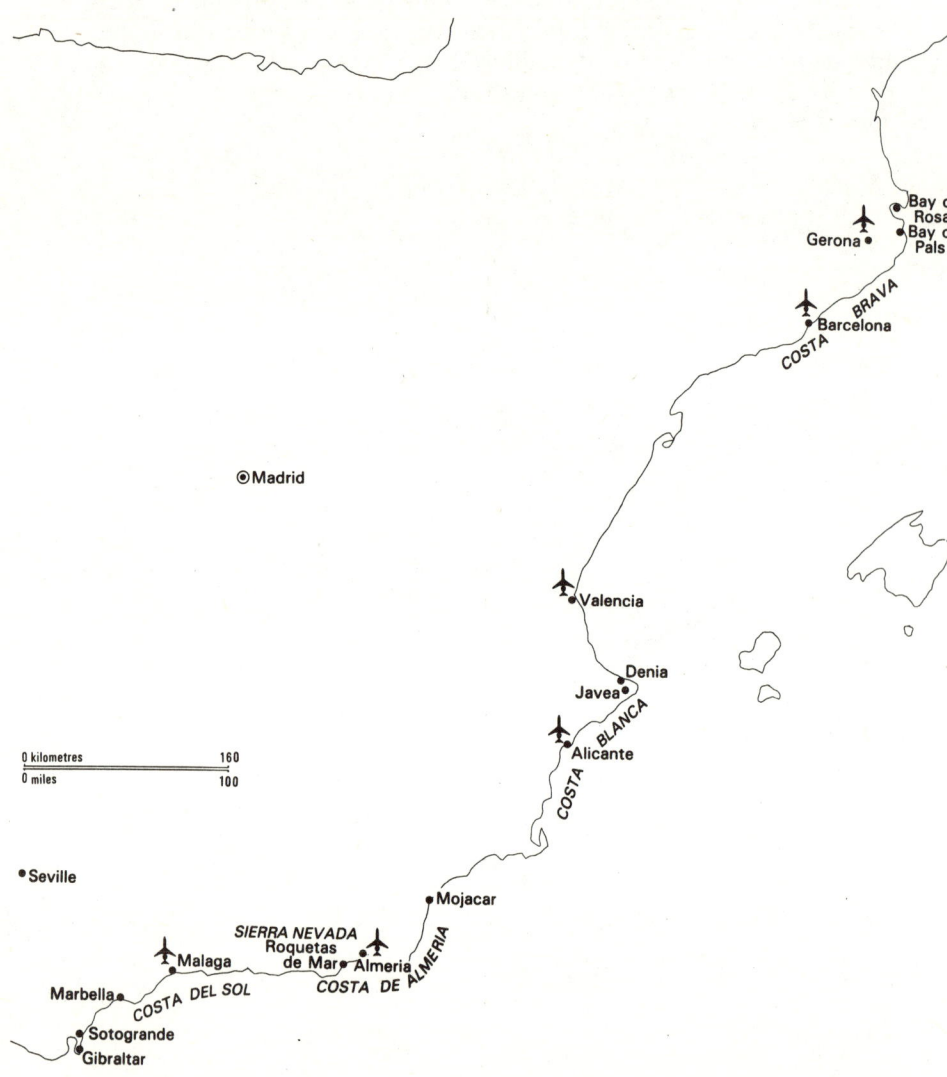

In any one year some 30 million pale-faced tourists visit Spain in search of the sun. A good many return to buy a property, and in recent years it has been the Brits who have been leading the way. Last year, around thirty thousand of us bought a property in Spain, either for holidays or for retirement.

Spain, more than any other country in Europe, is geared up for the foreign property buyer. Cheap and plentiful chartered flights ensure quick and easy access, and, until recently, property has been relatively inexpensive. Prices, naturally, have shot up with demand, but bargains can still be had if you select carefully, and the cost of living, too, can be relatively cheap if you live on a diet of booze and cigarettes and fresh local food. In addition, Spain's famous Costas – the Costa del Sol, the Costa Blanca, the Costa de Almeria and the Costa Brava – cater for any leisure pursuit you may care to follow: sailing, tennis, watersports and, of course, golf, to name just a few.

A country blessed with sunshine, it has long been an established destination for the tourist and holiday home buyer alike, but today it is also in the throes of a national revival, making it one of the most exciting countries in Europe both for native Spaniards and for foreigners investing in the country. A series of events have contributed. In February 1985, Spain saw the reopening of its frontier with Gibraltar, boosting confidence and accelerating plans to revitalize Spain's southern region, Andalucia. A year later, in January 1986, Spain joined the European Economic Community, and today, along with the rest of us, is preparing for the planned introduction of European law aimed at lessening trading and immigration barriers in 1992.

But 1992 is, for Spain, more than a Community target date. That year will be the five hundredth anniversary of Columbus's discovery of the New World, and in commemoration Seville, the capital of Andalucia, will be hosting the EXPO 92 world fair. In addition, Barcelona will be hosting the 1992 Olympics. Both events are being prepared for with engulfing enthusiasm. They represent a chance for the Spanish authorities to show off the delights of these two beautiful cities to the millions of visitors expected to attend from all over the world.

Costa del Sol

The Costa del Sol, the 'coast of the sun', lives up to its name with over three hundred days of sunshine a year. Stretched out between the high peaks of the Sierra Nevada and the Mediterranean, it has long, balmy summers, and the temperatures in winter rarely drop below 60°F. It is Spain's leading leisure resort, with year-round entertainment to rival any in the world.

Its pseudonym is the Costa del Golf. The coastal strip from Malaga airport to Gibraltar has no fewer than sixteen golf courses, many of them of championship standard. Severiano Ballesteros is a national hero. There are also numerous sports centres, tennis courts, sailing clubs and marinas, riding schools, two polo fields, even bowling greens; and if you want to snow-ski as well as water-ski, you can, on the slopes of Sol-y-Nieve in the Sierra Nevada.

The choice of property on the Costa del Sol is inexhaustible, with new 'urbanizations' of pueblos, villas and townhouses being continually added to the coastline's backdrop of hotels and residential developments. There are also splendid palaces and penthouses owned by Arab sheikhs, descendants of the Moors, who have begun a new invasion at the Costa's most salubrious centre – Marbella.

This vital, cosmopolitan town is the most fashionable resort on the coast. It is also the most expensive. The names above the shopfronts in Marbella can also be found in Paris or Milan, and a smart meal out for two costs about the same as in London. The beaches offer every conceivable type of watersport from windsurfing to sailing and water-skiing. Marbella isn't just a tourist resort, though: it's a financial centre with the latest in telecommunications and international couriers allowing business to carry on as usual, most frequently from the golf club or poolside bar.

It is difficult to find a small flat in Marbella for under £50,000, but there again few people are looking in this bracket. Most people attracted to Marbella want a villa, and generally they are not fussed what they pay for it. In Marbella, you pay your money and you take your choice. A six-bedroom, six-bathroom villa on the beach might cost around half a million pounds; a palace, £15 million. At a more modest level, a four-bedroomed furnished villa, for example, 100 yards from the beach, can cost around £130,000; a three-bedroom, three-bathroom villa on the golf course, with staff quarters and a pool, around £275,000.

No trip to Marbella is complete without sampling the nocturnal delights of Puerto Banus, otherwise known as the St Tropez of the Costa del Sol. At this extraordinary Andalucian-style marina development, the discos and piano bars play on until the late early hours of the morning. Those who want to join in the fun can pay upwards of £70,000 for a one-bedroom apartment in one of the residential complexes at Puerto Banus. Two- and three-bedroom units cost between £105,000 and £200,000.

There was a time when Marbella was in the centre of a continuous string of holiday homes stretching from the package tour resort of Torremolinos in the east to that of Estepona in the west. Now, with the Gibraltar frontier open, development has spread westwards beyond Estepona as far as the colony itself. Sotogrande, a vast 4400-acre residential estate, lies just 12 miles from the border.

Ten years ago, Sotogrande was a quiet, understated rural retreat, mainly for wealthy Spaniards escaping the city life. Today it is a sophisticated international resort with two golf courses, polo grounds, commercial and medical facilities, sports club and a marina – the largest on the Costa del Sol and the first on entering the Mediterranean from Gibraltar. There are also plans to construct by 1992 a sports complex equipped with training facilities and an injury clinic for professional sportsmen preparing for the Olympics.

More than anywhere on the Costa del Sol, Sotogrande has flourished as a result of the reopening of the Gibraltar frontier in 1985. Once a two-and-a-half-hour slog from Malaga airport along the notorious CN340 highway, it is now a painless twenty-minute hop from Gibraltar.

Not surprisingly, its new-found accessibility has been reflected in

property prices on the estate. When the frontier was reopened, some rose by 30 per cent overnight. Since then, there has been a steady growth of 10–15 per cent a year.

Properties at Sotogrande range from established luxury villas to building plots for custom-designed homes, beach apartments, and more recently apartments in Puerto Sotogrande's new marina complex. A marina apartment starts at £45,000 for a studio, rising to £320,000 for a four-bedroomed penthouse. It is rare for villas on the estate to be put up for sale; when they do they fall within a wide price range, depending on size and location. A three-bedroomed furnished villa with pool costs around £175,000; a five-bedroomed house close to the port, £325,000. Although property here is expensive, anyone with a house at Sotogrande can expect to be rewarded handsomely if they are prepared to rent it out. In the high season, a two-bed apartment can command £1000 a week; a four-bedroomed villa with pool, as much as £2500 a week. Alternatively, there is always an active long-term rental market for commuters working in Gibraltar.

The size and scale of Sotogrande are exceptional. The majority of developments along the coast are generally smaller, with a choice of apartments and pueblo village houses. Land prices for villas are often prohibitive. More often than not the architectural style is Andalucian with bright white walls, archways, balconies and marble throughout. Most developments have a communal swimming pool and many have a fitness centre or gymnasium.

Bearing in mind that a high proportion of foreigners living on the Costa del Sol are retired (over 60 per cent in Marbella are over sixty years old), many developers are now incorporating community centres, workshops, even allotments – an American initiative which should hopefully provide a welcome alternative to the expatriate bar. Some developments also include telex and fax facilities and conference rooms, so that residents, perhaps in semi-retirement, can remain active in business while enjoying the benefits of a sunny, health-giving climate. If you are considering an early retirement on the Costa, you should, however, beware of the 'ghost urbanization', the development geared to the holiday home buyer rather than the permanent resident that can become depressingly lifeless during the winter months.

The price of properties on the Costa, like anywhere, varies with location, size, quality and facilities offered on the development. Property in Estepona and Fuengirola is generally more reasonable than in Marbella or Sotogrande. Some developments, such as Dominion Beach and Club Miraflores, offer beach frontage, beautifully landscaped gardens, extravagant interiors and endless sporting activities, and are obviously sold at a premium. Others, back from the beach, are offered at more affordable prices.

Costa del Sol (excluding Marbella and Sotogrande)

	Sea views + communal pool (back from the beach)	Sea front or golf course
1 bed apartment	£25,000–40,000	£35,000–60,000
2 bed apartment	£35,000–60,000	£70,000–150,000
3 bed apartment/pueblo	£70,000–90,000	£100,000–200,000

Country properties

It is possible to select a development on the Costa del Sol where you can enjoy the sunshine and quality of life and hardly speak a word of Spanish. Many hardened Brits have lived for twenty years in Spain without adding more than a handful of Spanish words to their vocabulary. For those who care to look beneath the cosmopolitan veneer, old Spain can still be be found: flamenco guitars play next to their electric counterparts, and tapas bars still serve delicious arrays of spiced sausages and anchovies. For the real taste of Spain, though, you must leave behind the sun-strip coastline and head for the dazzling white villages and majestic landscape of inland Andalucia.

Perched high on the hilltops in Andalucia, only a short drive from

Gibraltar, the ancient frontier towns of Jerez de la Frontera, Jimena de la Frontera and many more are reminders of the Christian reconquest of Spain from the Moors in the early middle ages. Here lime-washed houses, narrow streets, arches and courtyards prevail, brightly splashed with ceramics and geraniums and cooled by sparkling fountains.

If you are prepared to invest some time and money, a small run-down house in one of these villages can be picked up for around £25,000 – much cheaper than on the coast. A three-bedroomed property with a pool and some land might cost around £120,000. Further from Gibraltar, yet only forty minutes' drive from Malaga, habitable village and country houses are cheaper still:

Country properties near the Costa del Sol

2 bed village house with patio	£25,000–30,000
3 bed village house with patio	£30,000–40,000
2 bed country house	£30,000–40,000
3 bed country house	£35,000–45,000
4 bed country house	£50,000–60,000
large country house + guest quarters	£100,000–200,000

Needless to say, it is essential to have a car if you are to choose a property away from the services on the coast. However, now is the time to make the effort if you are thinking of buying in this region. Vast sums of money are being invested to ensure that the EXPO 92 exhibition in Seville is a success. Large-scale road projects are being set in motion, airports enlarged and new hotels built for an anticipated 20 million visitors. The result will be an improved infrastructure and improved accessibility, highlighting the delights of this largely undiscovered part of Spain.

Costa de Almeria

Starting where the Costa del Sol ends, the Costa de Almeria stretches eastwards as far as the small, developing resort of Vera. The least developed of all Spain's Mediterranean seaboards, at least in tour operator terms, the Costa de Almeria nevertheless has its fair share of long golden beaches and residential developments – considerably cheaper than those on the Costa del Sol. It is easily accessible, with direct flights either to Malaga or the region's capital, Almeria.

Steeped in history, Almeria was, briefly, under Moorish occupation, the second wealthiest city in Europe after Constantinople. Its industry then was silk; today it is fish, market gardening and tourism. The old town has a wealth of ancient churches and fortresses, the most impressive of which is the Alcazaba, an enormous tenth-century fortress built by Aderraman III on the site of even earlier fortifications. Almeria remains, though, very much a Spanish town, with little nightlife besides a few bars and cafés around the harbour area. The vast expanses of shimmering plastic sheeting in the surrounding valleys are a sign that market gardening plays as important a role in Almeria's economy as tourism.

To the west of Almeria, about an hour's drive from the airport, lies the town, or rather two towns, of Mojacar. Mojacar splits neatly into the old Moorish village high on the hill, and Mojacar Playa, the new coastal resort stretched along the mile-long beach. The two provide a pleasant contrast: the old with steep cobbled streets, white cuboid houses spilling down the hillside, charming restaurants and bars; and the new with smart hotels, modern holiday developments, more restaurants and bars, and, of course, the gently sloping sandy beach.

Most of the residential developments are stretched out between the beach road and the hills: clusters of apartments, townhouses and villas, often built in traditional Moorish style with landscaped gardens and communal pools. Some are further back in the hills, set in a parched and barren landscape but nevertheless enjoying spectacular coastal views. Clint Eastwood fans may recognize the area as the setting for many a classic spaghetti western. For the sports-minded, there is an existing 9-hole golf course and two new courses – one 18-hole and one 27-hole – planned for the area. There is also a marina at the small fishing port of Garrucha, about four miles along the coast.

Mojacar

1 bed apartment	£15,000–30,000
2 bed apartment	£30,000–40,000
2 bed linked villa	£35,000–45,000
3 bed linked villa	£45,000–55,000
3 bed detached villa	£65,000–110,000

A little way around the Bay of Almeria to the west, about forty minutes' drive from the airport, is Roquetas, a small fishing harbour with just a handful of bars, a covered market and a few shops. A mile further on is Roquetas de Mar, an expanding purpose-built resort, no more than fifteen years old, which is already one of the largest resorts on the Costa de Almeria. It's a lively, international spot with several three- and four-star hotels, bars, restaurants and cafés. The beach, however, is long and narrow and mainly shingle – best suited, perhaps, for windsurfing. There is an 18-hole golf course and, about half an hour's drive away, a newly finished marina at Aguadulce.

The main residential area in Roquetas de Mar lies either side of the main thoroughfare, the Avenida Mediterraneo. Smart villas, often with private pools, are relatively dear for this stretch of coast. A four-bedroomed villa, for example, complete with pool, about 500 yards from the beach, might cost around £110,000; a spacious four-bedroomed villa with pool, overlooking the golf course, recently sold for £165,000. The beach area is mainly hotels and holiday apartments, some quite high-rise.

Roquetas de Mar

1 bed apartment	£20,000–30,000
2 bed apartment	£35,000–50,000
3 bed apartment	£50,000–65,000
2–3 bed detached villa	£85,000–120,000
4 bed detached villa	£100,000–170,000

Costa Blanca

With the exception of Benidorm, a package tour resort so famous that it has been the butt of comedians' jokes for the best part of a generation, the Costa Blanca is a region of moderate prices, low-rise developments and tight planning controls. Brits who buy holiday homes here tend to extend their stay and end up in permanent residence when they retire. Cheap and frequent flights from Alicante and Valencia ensure that they can make regular trips home to the mother country.

The most popular resorts are the old fishing villages of Denia and Javea in a part of the Costa Blanca called the 'Garden of Spain', a region famous for its fertile valleys of oranges and lemons and almond groves. Denia in particular is popular with the British, perhaps because of the link our forebears established in the days of Queen Victoria. They built a harbour and a packing plant and put Denia on the map as the centre of a thriving raisin industry, since when the locals have regarded us not as intruders, but as people who contributed to the prosperity of their town.

Steeped in history, Denia is one of the oldest ports on the Mediterranean coast. Its narrow streets and pretty lined avenues of shops and cafés are dominated by the ancient castle, and behind that Mount Mongo, an impressive mountain ridge that the locals affectionately refer to as the sleeping elephant. Denia has a fine stretch of sandy beach from where, on a clear day, it's possible to see all the way to Ibiza.

Some of the best buys in Denia are resale villas, many of them constructed in attractive honey-coloured Tosca stone. For around £70,000 you can buy a well-designed two-bedroomed villa with about a quarter of an acre of land. A three-bedroomed villa would cost around £100,000. Although planning controls are strict in the area, a few carefully controlled developments are still being constructed. A studio flat, for instance, a quarter of an hour's walk from the beach, costs around £26,000; a two-bedroomed townhouse, between £46,000 and £55,000.

A few miles south along the coast, still in the shadow of the magnificent

QUALITY HOMES ON THE COSTA BLANCA

Beaches International Property have sold a fine range of new and resale property on the Costa Blanca for ten years. There are hundreds of clients holidaying or living permanently in the resorts around the Cabo de la Nao headland who are testament to the quality of service they have enjoyed from the Company.

Superb freehold property is available in this most beautiful area of Spain, much of which is protected as a Conservation Area. Property in the coastal towns and villages of Javea, Moraira, El Portet, Calpe and Altea, or inland in the fertile Jalon Valley, can be purchased from £30,000 to £300,000. There are luxurious villas, beautifully located holiday homes sharing their own swimming pool, apartments close to or looking on to an expanse of sandy beach.

The quality of advice and product knowledge provided by Beaches is second to none and this service is available to clients free of charge through management teams based in the UK and in Spain. Service is provided in conjunction with, but independently of the developers for whom Beaches act.

Service provides for property viewing, travel arrangements, legal and financial advice, letting advice, furnishing – every aspect of purchasing and after sales service.

Visit our permanent exhibition at Hagley Hall
or write or telephone for details

BEACHES INTERNATIONAL PROPERTY, 3/4 HAGLEY MEWS, HAGLEY HALL, HAGLEY, WEST MIDLANDS DY9 9LQ

Associated Companies: Beaches International Travel – Members of ABTA
Beaches Financial Services – Appointed Representatives of Hill Samuel

Beaches — telephone: 0562 885181

---

sleeping elephant, lies Javea with its colourful port and bustling marina. The old town, with its narrow streets and whitewashed walls and imposing fortress church, lies separate, about a half-mile inland. It's worthy of note that Javea has been declared by the World Health Organization as being 'environmentally near perfect'. Certainly it is the first of Spain's resorts to catch the morning sun and it enjoys the longest hours of daylight.

Traditionally Javea has been a peaceful destination for many retired visitors to spend a relaxing summer break, or even the best part of the winter, comparatively cheaply by British standards. As in Denia, some of the best buys are villas, new or resale, often built in traditional Moorish style with archways and tapering chimneys. A two-bedroomed villa can cost as little as £60,000–70,000. In the Arenal beach area, surrounding a wide horseshoe of golden sand, two- and three-bedroomed apartments can be bought for between £45,000 and £70,000.

Inland, prices can be considerably cheaper. In the Jalon valley, for instance, a beautiful and fertile garden of oranges, lemons and vines about ten miles from the coast, a two-bedroomed villa costs around £55,000; a three-bedroomed villa, £65,000. Original *fincas*, old Spanish farmhouses, usually on an acre or two of land, can also be found for between £40,000 and £60,000. At least twice the purchase price should be allowed, though, for conversion and modernization.

Denia and Javea

1 bed apartment	£30,000–35,000
2 bed apartment	£40,000–55,000
3 bed apartment	£45,000–70,000
2 bed villa	£60,000–90,000
3 bed villa	£80,000–200,000

The Costa Blanca also serves the golf enthusiast. Behind Mount Mongo, about five miles inland at La Sella, a championship golf course is being constructed under the professional eye of José Maira Olazabal, Spain's young hopeful tipped to mature into a Ballesteros. Shares in the golf club are being sold exclusively to owners of the surrounding properties. Apartments, mostly with panoramic views across to the Bay of Velensia, start at £35,000. Three-bedroomed townhouses roll in at £72,000 and four-bedroomed villas with pools at £200,000.

For golf, though, it is difficult to compete with the 1,600-acre La Manga estate. It has three golf courses, soon to be four, as well as a David Lloyd tennis centre, squash and swimming and a cricket pitch – a hint that La Manga caters exclusively for the British. It also has a private beach, a four-star hotel and a choice of properties ranging from one-bedroomed apartments at £45,000 to six-bedroomed villas at £450,000.

Costa Brava

The Costa Brava or 'rugged coast', running south from the French–Spanish border to just north and east of Barcelona, is well known among package tour holiday makers. Resorts such as San Felio, Tossa and Lloret de Mar can be found in any Spanish holiday brochure you might happen to browse through. But, as in so many areas, these popular resorts serve to satisfy a mass need for sun, sea and sand, while preserving the remaining coastline for those prepared to venture off the beaten track. Much of the coastline, as its name suggests, is still staggeringly beautiful with red-brown headlands and Mediterranean pine forests reaching down to sheltered sandy coves.

Catalonia, the north-eastern region, is richly irrigated by rivers flowing from the Pyrenees. The rolling countryside is lush and green; agriculture as well as manufacturing provides a sound economic base, while art and culture are still very much alive. Catalonia was the training ground for Picasso, Salvador Dali and the architect Gaudi.

So close to France, the northern stretch of the Costa Brava in particular provides an excellent alternative for home buyers who, if they had more money in their pockets, might opt for the south of France. The sea is blue, if not bluer (it has been voted the cleanest in Europe), the food is as mouth-watering and the travelling time much the same. One friend reputedly drove from the Channel ports to Spain in five minutes under ten hours, though twelve hours might be considered good going for a more sober individual. Alternatively, you can fly to Gerona or Barcelona.

Setting it apart from the south of France, or from any other part of Europe for that matter, Barcelona, the capital of Catalonia, is the chosen location for the 1992 Olympics. Although property is considerably cheaper here than on the Costa del Sol, prices in Catalonia have been shooting up by 20–25 per cent a year. The Olympics, together with strict planning controls in the area, can be expected to push up property prices still further in this region.

The variety of properties in Catalonia is enormous: ancient village houses, old farmhouses, newly built villas on golf courses and apartments overlooking marinas. In Bagur, for example, a village dominated by its eighth-century castle set a few miles from the sea, a small two-bedroomed cottage in need of a lick of paint can be picked up for around £40,000. A modern four-bedroomed villa overlooking the same village costs around £75,000; a fully renovated stone *masia* (farmhouse) in three acres of land with four bedrooms, huge open fireplaces and solid wooden beams, around £180,000.

Life in the Catalan countryside requires a splattering of Spanish. But in return for your efforts you will be received warmly by the locals, and be spoilt with sizzling displays of wholesome country cooking: duck with turnips, rabbit in rum, partridge, hare and roast boar are all delicious Catalan dishes eaten straight from the wood-fired ovens of many a village restaurant.

Down on the coast there are a number of purpose-built golfing and leisure developments well away from the package tours of Tossa and Lloret. One of the most prestigious is at Playa de Pals, a superb sandy beach that stretches for miles around the entire Bay of Pals. Just back from the beach is the championship Pals Golf Club, around which selective holiday home development is taking place. A furnished two-bedroom, two-bathroom apartment costs between £65,000 and £70,000.

Just a couple of miles from the golf course is the ancient village of Pals itself. Forty years ago it lay in ruins, deserted; but now, after complete renovation, its medieval castle and fortified walls stand proudly overlooking the sea. Once again people walk the old cobbled streets and work in the surrounding fields.

Further north, close to the border with France, the fishing villages of Llansa and Cadaques offer a charming blend of Gallic and Spanish. In the summer months, Llansa overflows with hordes of weekend visitors from just across the border. Cadaques, on the other hand, is a quieter spot. A collection of cuboid white houses clustered around a fishing harbour, it should, with luck, be protected from a concrete invasion by strict planning controls imposed in the area. Both villages offer a selection of some of the best restaurants in Spain.

Moving southwards into the Bay of Rosas, there are one or two complexes that have been developed specifically with the holidaymaker in mind. There is, for example, a yachting centre that has been sensitively developed over a period of twenty-five years or so. It has a total of 20 miles of navigable canals, lined with private moorings and waterside homes. Prices start at £28,000 for a one-bedroom apartment, rising to between £500,000 and £700,000 for a luxury home with private berth.

At the southern tip of the Bay of Rosas is La Escala, a town famous worldwide for its anchovies. It's a lively town with bars and nightclubs, a marina and superb sandy beach, and, of course, a large fishing fleet which supplies a daily market and the local restaurants. It's a good choice for a holiday residence or for a more permanent home. A three-bedroomed home could be picked up in La Escala for between £60,000 and £80,000.

Just outside La Escala are the historic remains of Ampurias, once the centre of Roman colonization in the area. It is here, in 1992, that the Olympic flame will arrive on Spanish soil for the last leg of its journey to Barcelona for the Olympic Games.

Costa Brava (coastal properties)

1 bed apartment	£30,000–40,000
2 bed apartment	£35,000–60,000
2 bed villa	£60,000–100,000
3 bed villa	£70,000–120,000

Buying

The popularity of Spain as a holiday destination and the speed at which property has been developed to cater for the overseas buyer has inevitably resulted in a few casualties along the way. The sheer scale of development and the number of purchasers involved have probably resulted in Spain suffering a worse press than any other country in Europe. In a number of cases fault has been shown to lie with an unscrupulous developer or agent, but it has to be said that part of the blame often lies with the purchaser. For some reason, normally level-headed people, who take sensible precautions when buying a property at home, develop a reckless disregard for the same needs when buying a property abroad. It cannot be stressed enough that, when buying a property, old or new, it is essential to employ a solicitor with a practical working knowledge of Spanish law.

If you buy a property from a developer, you might well be asked to sign an option or contract of reservation, usually against the payment of a small deposit. If so, make quite sure the deposit is returnable if you decide not to go ahead.

The first legally binding document you will be asked to sign, whether buying from a developer or from an individual, is a private contract of sale, or *contracto privado de compra ventra*. This document sets out details of the property, the agreed price, the payment terms and the intended date of completion. Signing the contract is equivalent to the exchange of contracts in England and inevitably requires immediate payment of a non-refundable deposit – usually amounting to 10 per cent of the purchase price.

Before committing yourself in this way, ensure that your solicitor undertakes a full title search. He should check there are no mortgages registered on the property, that the vendor has no outstanding taxes to pay and that the proper planning permission has been obtained from the necessary authorities. This last point takes on a greater importance in the light of recent reports that the Spanish government intended to nationalize properties built without planning permission.

If the property is part of an estate or block of flats, a copy of the co-ownership rules should be obtained: if the development is still undergoing construction, rigorous enquiries should be made to establish the financial standing of the developer and to ensure the building programme is adequately funded.

The usual period between signing the private contract and completion is a month. Transfer of the title deeds (*escritura de compra venta*) is carried out before the local notary (*notario publico*) with the vendor and purchaser – or representatives having their power of attorney – signing the relevant documents. Before a transfer can be completed, it is essential to produce a bank certificate showing that the necessary funds have been imported into Spain through an authorized Spanish bank. This satisfies Spanish exchange control regulations and ensures there will be no problems when it comes to repatriation of funds on resale of the property.

Payment of the relevant purchase costs takes place on signing the *escritura*. These include notary's fees, registration expenses and IVA (Spanish VAT) payable at 6 per cent on villas and apartments and 12 per cent on building plots. Broadly speaking, these costs amount to 8 per cent of the purchase price for a villa or apartment, 14 per cent for a building plot. Note that in Spain it is a criminal offence to underdeclare the purchase price on an *escritura*. An additional 1–1½ per cent should be put aside for legal fees. After payment, the *escritura* is officially registered in the local property register.

Selling

Repatriation of funds on selling a property in Spain is not a problem provided the funds for the original purchase were imported into Spain through the correct banking channels. As may be expected, Capital Gains Tax is levied on any profit made on the sale. This varies depending on resident status. In addition a local value added tax *plus valia*, based on the increased value of the land since the last change of ownership was registered, will be levied. Although in theory this should be paid by the vendor, in practice it is often carried by the purchaser. The amount varies on locality and the length of time since the last registration.

Company ownership

An important matter for which you will almost certainly need professional advice is the name in which you register your new property. Your decision will be mainly influenced by tax considerations, in particular inheritance tax and capital gains tax on death or resale of your Spanish property.

Traditionally, the property would be registered in your sole name or in the joint names of you and your spouse. An increasingly popular method, however, is to register it in the name of an offshore company. This method is widely practised because it provides a perfectly legal way to avoid Spanish capital gains tax and inheritance tax. In effect it means that, after the initial purchase, the property does not change hands on resale or on death; instead the shares in the company are sold or inherited.

Despite avoiding Spanish taxes, however, this method of purchase does incur costs. Estimates vary, but around £1000 to set up a company offshore and another £500 a year to run it might be a fair guide. Whether or not the tax savings will justify the expense of an offshore company will depend on the value of the property and the status of the individual purchaser.

CHAPTER 4
THE BALEARICS

One of Europe's best-publicized holiday areas, the Balearic islands, scattered off the east coast of Spain, are becoming increasingly popular with the foreign property buyer. Easy access from Britain, a warm climate, sweeping bays and varied and beautiful countryside make the islands an ideal location for a holiday apartment or more permanent residence. Mallorca is the largest and the best known, but Menorca and Ibiza also offer a wide range of properties to suit all pockets.

Mallorca

Few people think of Mallorca without conjuring up an image of low-budget package tours, fish and chips and the kiss-me-quick hat brigade. This, however, is just one side of Mallorca, blown up out of all proportion by bad press coverage of one or two over-commercialized resorts covering a tiny fraction of the 200 miles of rich and varied coastline.

The truth is that people in the know have kept quiet about its hidden charms; also its golf courses and marinas. There are as many yachts in Mallorca as along the French Riviera. Generations of wealthy Madrid families have made Mallorca their second home, and for years it has been the chosen summer retreat of the King of Spain. Not once, but twice, Charles and Diana have joined him.

Mallorca's scenery is as diverse as its visitors. An island just 3640 square miles, its terrain is as varied as a continent's. Rugged mountains in the west alternate with gentle rolling hills and a vast and windy central plain dappled with fruit orchards and windmills. For yachtsmen, few coastlines in Europe can match its north-westerly coast, where dramatic cliffs alternate with a succession of hidden coves accessible only from the sea. Midway between Cabo Formentor in the north and Puerto de Andraitx in the south, Puerto de Soller provides a welcome refuge from the challenging sea.

A drive along hair-raising bends twisting through the dramatic west coast scenery will lead you to some of the most picturesque and unspoilt villages on the island: Banyalbufar, for instance, Deia, Estellencs or Valldemosa, a favoured retreat of the composer Chopin. As pretty as they may be these mountain villages do not offer the beaches and gentle waters so popular with the majority of summer tourists and property buyers. For these, head for the sunny south-west corner around Palma Bay, the northern corner around Alcudia, or the eastern coast from Cala Santania to Cala Ratjuda.

Among a population of a million islanders, fifty thousand British folk have made Mallorca their permanent home. Property is no longer cheap; it has been going up steadily by around 10 per cent a year and in some cases by as much as 30 per cent a year. Tighter planning controls – such as the 100-metre rule, common to the whole of Spain, which no longer permits development within 100 metres of the coastline – could push prices up still further. Mallorca remains, though, one of the most accessible holiday destinations in Europe; its airport is the second busiest in Europe after Heathrow. Wherever you might choose to spend a holiday or buy a property on the island, it will be within an hour and a half's drive of landing at Palma.

Magalluf to El Arenal

The short stretch of coast from Magalluf through the capital, Palma, to El Arenal is the most densely populated and commercially developed on the island. It is pockets within this stretch that have earned Mallorca its lager lout image. Every form of entertainment is on offer: discos, bars, nightclubs, twenty-four-hour fast food.

Situated almost on the runway of Palma airport, conveniently close for the weekly coach loads of package tour holidaymakers, El Arenal is the Torremolinos of Mallorca – although in fairness, steps are being taken to smarten up its image. Here, and in Magalluf, a one-bed flat in a block of apartments could be picked up for as little as £25,000, a two-bedder for around £30,000.

Magalluf to El Arenal

1 bed apartment	£25,000–35,000
2 bed apartment	£30,000–40,000
3 bed apartment	£40,000–60,000

There is hardly an area the size of a postage stamp left for more luxurious holiday homes along this stretch of the coast, with the exception, perhaps, of one or two developments, the most notable of which is Bendinat.

The 850-acre Bendinat estate just west of Palma sells itself as 'the other Mallorca', and is top of the new-image market on the island. Central to the estate is the Anchorage Club, run by Prince Alfonso von Hohenlohe, founder of the famous Marbella Club. It has a restaurant, piano bar, library, swimming pool, even a small private beach, and exudes a feeling of exclusivity. Clustered around the club is the Anchorage Village, a pleasing group of old-style Mallorcan houses comprising one-, two- and three-bedroomed apartments selling at exclusive prices starting at £235,000. Colour-washed in faded pastel shades, with the old enclosed balcony, pillars and archways, wooden shutters and old tiled roofs, the village offers a feeling of antiquity despite being just a few years old. The architect is François Spoerry, creator of Port Grimaud in the south of France.

On another part of the estate there are more royal connections at the golf club. Bendinat's Royal Golf Club, with 9-hole course soon to be 18, has King Juan Carlos as its Honorary President. Golf apartments alongside the fairway start at £70,000 for a one-bedder rising to £150,000 for a three-bedroomed apartment. There are also detached villas and plots of land available for sale on the estate.

West of Magalluf

The premium price commanded for the little land remaining around Palma has forced developers to look west young man, beyond Magalluf to the rocky peninsula south-west of Palma Bay and further west to Camp de Mar and Puerto de Andraitx. This area, with new marinas, golf courses and smart garden developments, still within easy access of the capital and the airport, probably offers the best investment opportunity on the island.

At Santa Ponsa, for instance, once a sleepy Mallorcan village, there is now a golf course with a second one under construction and a third on the drawing board. There is also a proposed 700-berth marina. A smart new marina bordered by village-style shops and restaurants has already been constructed at Puerto Portals, adding to the somewhat select yachting marina at Club de Mar.

Development is underway at Cala Viñas and Camp de Mar, both small resorts offering soft, sandy beaches in contrast to the surrounding rugged coastline; and at Puerto de Andraitx, the longest-established holiday destination in this south-western corner. In common with so many ports in Mallorca, Puerto de Andraitx is a mile or so from the original inland town of the same name. Rising steeply in terraces above Puerto de Andraitx towards Andraitx itself, apartments and villas overlook the charming old harbour and sea beyond.

A number of small garden developments, characteristically with clustered buildings around a central pool, are springing up in this area. As a rule, they don't come cheap. A two-bedroomed apartment starts at around £60,000, a three-bedroomed apartment at around £80,000. Sea views and proximity to a golf course can push up the price, so that a four- or five-bedroomed villa at Santa Ponsa could fetch up to half a million pounds. Generally, though, prices fall within the following brackets.

West of Magalluf

2 bed apartment	£60,000–80,000
3 bed apartment	£80,000–115,000
4 bed penthouse	£200,000–300,000
3 bed detached house, inland	£110,000–200,000
4 bed detached house, inland	£225,000–300,000

Puerto Pollensa and Puerto Alcudia

An hour's drive north of Palma, Puerto Pollensa and Puerto Alcudia once again illustrate the two contrasting faces of Mallorca. In this northern corner of the island you can buy a studio in an aparthotel for £20,000 or a palatial mansion worth millions.

Perhaps the most enchanting retreat, for those who can afford it, is Formentor. A tranquil spot, built on high land overlooking the Bay of Pollensa, it centres around the old-established five-star Formentor Hotel. In the good old days, the magnificent villas surrounding the hotel were serviced as if they were extended luxury suites of the same establishment. Inhabitants relied totally on the hotel for electricity, post and telephone. Today, dependence has been reduced to water supplies and entertainment – unless, that is, the owners drive along the twisty road to Puerto Pollensa.

With restaurants, discos, bars and shops, Puerto Pollensa has developed directly in response to the holidaymakers who swarm to its magnificent sandy beach. It also has a 9-hole golf course. In Puerto Pollensa itself there are a number of apartments, some in blocks and some in garden developments, catering specifically for this holiday market, while the surrounding hills contain larger detached houses catering for a nucleus of permanent British inhabitants. These properties enjoy magnificent views of the bay.

Puerto Pollensa

1 bed apartment	£30,000–35,000
2 bed apartment	£45,000–70,000
3 bed apartment	£60,000–120,000
4 bed detached house	£300,000–450,000

Just a few miles around the corner at Puerto Alcudia you could only consider buying an apartment for holiday use, not for living in permanently. Like Puerto Pollensa, Puerta Alcudia has a magnificent sandy beach that draws the Germans, Scandinavians and British in their hordes, but it has been heavily built up with apartment blocks sometimes scaling ten storeys or more. The majority of properties for sale are one- and two-bedroom flats, either in blocks or aparthotels geared at the self-catering market. Houses are few and far between, although there are a handful of developments comprising small two- and three-bedroomed bungalows, again geared at the holiday market rather than permanent residence. Generally, prices are much cheaper than at its neighbouring resort.

Puerto Alcudia

studio apartment	£15,000–20,000
1 bed apartment	£20,000–25,000
2 bed apartment	£25,000–30,000
2–3 bed bungalow	£30,000–40,000

Cala Santanyi to Cala Ratjada

In contrast to the north and west of the island, the eastern coast, stretching from Cala Santanyi in the south up to Cala Ratjada, is flat, with creeky inlets and sandy beaches bordered by sweet-smelling pines. A good hour's drive from Palma, there are no major developments along this coast, rather a string of ports and marinas and smaller developments often constructed in Ibizan style, painted white with flat roofs and terraces.

Of the hundreds of Calas – Cala Figuera, Cala Marsal, Cala Morlanda, to name but a few – the one that has really taken off is Cala d'Or. Built around a marina and boasting the all-important golf course, Cala d'Or grows visibly larger by the year. Here you can pay anything from £40,000 up to £300,000. Generally the rather grander houses are on the northern side of town, while in the south the land is carpeted with modern holiday developments comprising two- and three-bedroom apartments and bungalows, usually with a communal pool.

Cala Santanyi to Cala Ratjada

2 bed apartment	£45,000–60,000
3 bed apartment	£60,000–85,000
3 bed holiday bungalow	£60,000–85,000
spacious 3 bed bungalow with pool	£85,000–110,000

Country properties

For more permanent living it is often more desirable to be away from the holiday resorts on the coast, either in an old country house or in a village. There was a time when you could pick up an old farm stable or barn for next to nothing, but those days have long gone. You won't find anything close to the activity in Palma, but if you persevere long enough you might find something further out, bearing in mind that by the time you have renovated it it could be considerably more expensive than buying a new property of an equivalent size. If it is outside a village it is unlikely to have mains water or drainage.

There is, of course, the option of buying a farmhouse that has already been converted. Often these feature huge entrance halls with big open fireplaces, exposed beams, flagstoned floors and courtyards. They ooze character and may come with several acres of land that usually would be let out to a local farmer. Farmhouses vary in price enormously, depending on their size, and most importantly, their accessiblity. You are unlikely, however, to find anything for under £150,000 – for which you might get a small three-bedroomed house with perhaps a couple of acres of land. For a larger property, close to the town, with a swimming pool and garden, you can expect to pay £400,000 or £500,000.

Country properties in Mallorca

3 bed country house	£150,000–250,000
4 bed country house	£200,000–400,000
5–6 bed country house	£400,000–600,000

Menorca

There is a school of thought that the Spanish keep the best for themselves. This is surely true of Menorca. A small island, just 30 miles across, its countryside is gentle and rolling, its beaches clean and often deserted. In contrast to many holiday areas in Spain, Menorca is surprisingly undeveloped. There are rural areas with grazing cattle and dry stone walls still approachable only along rough cart tracks, and beaches only accessible by foot. It's a perfect spot for families with young children or for those considering early retirement.

Generally speaking, the island can be divided north and south. The northern side is undulating, with hills and plans giving way to a rugged coastline with hidden beaches and sheltered inlets – perfect for windsurfing and diving. The southern side of the island is flatter, with bays and coves as well as long stretches of magnificent sandy beach. Son Bou beach, for instance, slopes gently into blue, blue waters for over a mile and a half.

The only land feature of any note is Monte Toro, a mountain, or more accurately a hill, nearly 1200 feet high with a monastery perched on top. Up here it is easy to see why Menorca has the reputation of being windy at times in the winter. In the summer, the climate is truly Mediterranean.

Like many parts of Spain, Menorca has been influenced by various races who have occupied the country in past generations – not least the British, who occupied Menorca for a total of sixty-six years in the eighteenth and early nineteenth centuries. Today, evidence of this occupation is still apparent, most of all in the architecture. Examples of Palladian façades introduced by the British, painted in their favourite colour, red, and picked out in white, can be seen scattered all over the island. In Villa Carlos, a town founded by the British and originally called Georgetown, the old houses are arranged geometrically around a military parade square, a far cry from the traditional Menorcan focus of the Catholic church.

Menorca has been the chosen spot for a select group of property buyers for a number of years. Many of the Menorcan country houses are British-owned, and now a growing number of holiday home buyers are attracted by the new residential developments springing up on the island. In the last couple of years demand has exceeded supply and prices have increased by 15–20 per cent a year. The cost of living, too, has shot up, so that a three-course meal with wine now costs around £15 a head.

With increasing popularity, so access to the island has become easier. There are now direct charter flights to the island's refurbished airport just south of the capital, Mahon, in the winter months as well as the summer. Alternatively, you can fly to Palma and change to a domestic flight, or, if you want your car, drive to Barcelona and take the ferry. A car, whether it's your own or hired, is essential if you are to enjoy the island to the full. Buses run between the principal towns, but not necessarily to and from the beaches and developments.

Country properties

Traditional Menorcan farmhouses, scrubbed white with green shutters and red-tiled roofs, are always in demand on the island, particularly in the south-eastern corner around Mahon and Villa Carlos. Few come on the market, however, and when they do they are snapped up before the casual buyer has a look in. To compete among the bidders you must have at least £100,000 in your pocket for a modest three-bedroomed property.

A rambling farmhouse with perhaps eight bedrooms, outbuildings and several acres of land can cost up to £500,000.

Many people opt to buy a plot and build themselves, although this too is becoming increasingly difficult as land is in short supply. The total cost of constructing a four-bedroomed property on, say, half an acre of land is £100,000–130,000.

New developments

New properties on the island are principally on small developments of apartments and villas, often in cluster buildings with communal gardens and swimming pools. In general, they are constructed for use as holiday homes rather than for permanent living. Planning controls are strict; most are low-rise and low-density.

The main areas of development are in the south and south-east corner, close to the airport and the social and commercial goings-on of Mahon and Villa Carlos. There are also some around Cuidadela in the west, although this region has never been as popular with British tourists.

Mahon, with its magnificent harbour and narrow streets, and Villa Carlos, just a mile and a half from the capital at the entrance of the harbour, both offer a lively selection of shops, supermarkets and restaurants, while retaining an old-fashioned charm. Properties are available in the towns themselves and in surrounding residential developments.

One of the first resorts to be developed on the island was Cala'n Porter, a lively and popular holiday spot about eight miles from the capital. As well as a healthy selection of restaurants and bars, it has a nightclub built spectacularly into the side of the rock. The beach at Cala'n Porter can be crowded by Menorcan standards.

S'Algar and San Jaime are both examples of residential estates along this southern strip. Typically, they have shops, boutiques, restaurants and bars to cater for their temporary residents. San Jaime is situated on Son Bou beach, the longest stretch of sand on the island.

The northern coast is less developed than the south, although a few noteworthy developments have sprung up in the last few years. One of the most acclaimed is the Menorca Country Club, a residential estate of traditional whitewashed villas and apartments built on a stretch of rocky coast near the old fishing village of Fornells. The Club itself has a restaurant and bar, tennis, swimming, gym and sub-aqua facilities. Diving in the crystal-clear waters is a popular pastime.

Also popular with sports-lovers is Son Parc, an estate on the northern coast, again near Fornells, which boasts the only golf course on the island. It also has a long, sandy bay surrounded by pine forest, but construction of villas and apartments has so far been very limited.

Generally speaking, the price of property is much the same in all parts of the island, with the exception perhaps of Cala'n Porter where a small two-bedroomed villa can still be picked up for around £35,000. Elsewhere £30,000 or £35,000 would be the rock-bottom price for a two-bedroomed flat. Prices vary, of course, with quality and amenities offered, but in most cases the starting price for a two-bed holiday apartment is nearer £40,000 or £50,000. Studio and one-bedroomed flats are few and far between. Because there are few hotels on the island, the rental market is active from April to the end of October.

New developments in Menorca

2 bed apartment	£40,000–45,000
2 bed villa	£50,000–60,000
3 bed villa	£80,000–120,000
4 bed villa	£120,000–160,000

Ibiza

The third largest and most southerly of the Balearic islands, Ibiza, just 25 miles from northern tip to south, boasts the best weather and some of the best beaches in the archipelago. Perhaps because of the warmth of the sunshine, and the tolerance and hospitality of its island people, who have seen numerous civilizations – ancient and modern – pass through its land, Ibiza has earned itself the reputation of being a non-conformist island. In Ibiza, anything goes. Dress the way you want, or not at all (there are two nudist beaches on the island), but make sure it's in good taste. The island is a favourite of the Germans and bronzed, blond Scandinavians.

Away from the beach, Ibiza is a refreshingly green island with large areas of woodland cladding its hilly terrain. The Greeks called it Pitiusa, meaning 'pine-covered', but there are also almond, fig and twisted olive trees, as well as tropical palms. Ancient Arab water-wheels and windmills are dotted prettily across the landscape.

In contrast the coastal resorts of San Antonio, Santa Eulalia del Rio and Ibiza town are packed with restaurants, bars and exceptional nightclubs. Around four thousand British people choose to live permanently on Ibiza, many in the inland country areas, just visiting the coastal towns for shopping and entertainment. It may be an alternative way of life, away from the stresses of the Western world, but the cost of living is much the same as in England. The heating bills may not be as astronomical, but a good meal out costs around £15 a head, and if you want to dance the night away it costs between £10 and £20 just to get in through the doors of one of the island's famous nightclubs.

Travelling to the island is easy in the summer months, with direct flights from London taking around two hours. From October through to March, though, flights from London to Ibiza involve a stopover at Barcelona. Alternatively, you can drive and catch the ferry from Barcelona, Valencia, Denia or Marseille.

Most of the holiday activity centres around Ibiza town and San Antonio, both bustling resorts teeming with sun 'n' fun worshippers in the summer months. Some ten miles north of Ibiza town on the eastern coast lies Santa Eulalia del Rio, a smaller, less pretentious town, still with restaurants and discos, but without unbearable crowds. It's here that many British people choose to buy an apartment or villa, both for holiday use and for permanent residence. The town lies at the mouth of the only river in the Balearics, surrounded by wooded hills. It's a favourite with writers and artists. Among its old buildings is one of the finest fortress-churches on the island, and there is a beach right in the centre of town. It's within easy access of the airport and close to the only golf course on the island.

In the town itself, most of the properties available are apartments in small blocks, some old, some new, some with front-line positions on the seafront. A very smart L-shaped block, for instance, with palm trees in a central court, right on the edge of the marina, has a selection of fully furnished two-bedroomed apartments for between £50,000 and £63,000. An older block, in need of a lick of paint but in an excellent position on the seafront, has one-bedroomed apartments selling at between £22,000 and £28,000, three-bedroomed apartments at £75,000. Just out of town, smaller resorts such as Cala Llonga, Cala San Vicente, Es Cana and Figueral offer a range of apartments and villas, often with a communal pool, at prices slightly below those in Santa Eulalia itself.

Ibiza

1 bed apartment	£25,000–30,000
2 bed apartment	£28,000–50,000
3 bed apartment	£45,000–80,000
2–3 bed villa	£75,000–150,000
4–5 bed villa	£100,000–250,000

Country properties
Some of the best buys on the island are the Ibizan cuboid villas, hidden away in colourful gardens in the wooded hills. Traditionally a family built a single dwelling of solid stone, adding more rooms only when finance allowed or a growing family beckoned. The result is a delightful huddle of different sized cubes, whitewashed with beamed roofs of savina wood, gracefully following the natural contours of the land. These ancient country properties make delightful modern homes, and set the style for newly constructed villas on the island.

The price of villas varies enormously with size and quality of finish. A few come on the market at £70,000 or £80,000, but generally £100,000 is the bottom price, rising to £300,000 or even £400,000. A partly converted three-bedroomed farmhouse, for instance, on roughly ten acres, set high overlooking the surrounding countryside, costs, £125,000; a modern villa on a quarter-acre plot, with four bedrooms and a good-sized swimming pool overlooking the wooded valleys and sea beyond, £165,000.

Country properties on Ibiza

3 bed country villa	£100,000–150,000
4 bed country villa	£150,000–250,000
4 bed country villa + guest wing	£250,000–400,000

Buying and Selling

Spanish law applies – see pages 49–51.

CHAPTER 5
CANARY ISLANDS

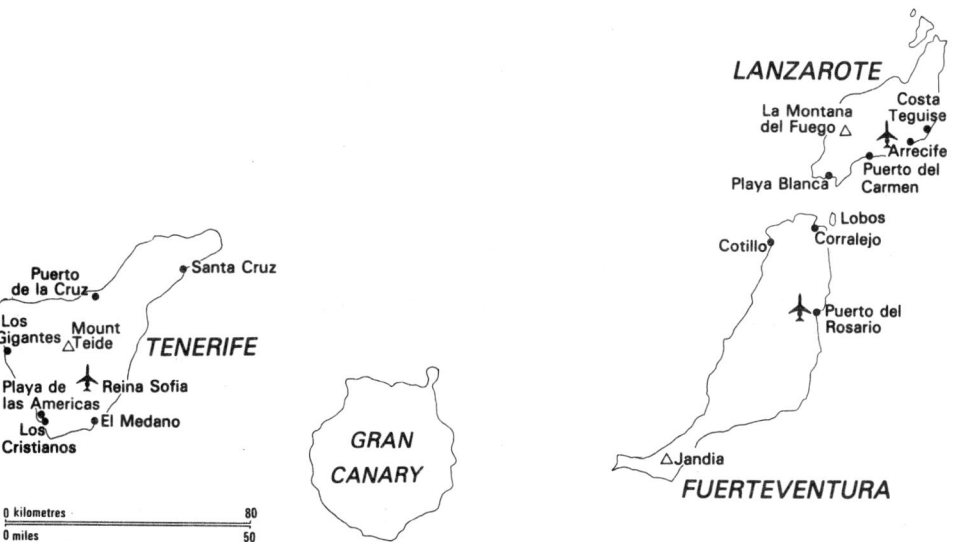

Unquestionably, the overwhelming attraction of the Canary Islands is the guaranteed winter sun. Further from Madrid than Madrid is from London, this Spanish archipelago off the coast of Morocco is on almost the same latitude as the Bahamas.

In total, there are seven islands and numerous islets in the Canaries. All share a common geological origin, having risen from the depths of the ocean in a series of volcanic eruptions. Each island, however, has its own distinctive beauty, its own character and its own attractions for the growing number of tourists who visit each year. For the home buyer, the most popular islands are Tenerife, Lanzarote and the newly discovered – in commercial terms – Fuerteventura.

Compared with mainland Spain, property on the islands, and the cost of living too, has traditionally been considered inexpensive. The islands are customs-free, making shopping for spirits, tobacco, perfume, watches and a range of electrical goods an unprecedented pleasure. However, in the tourist areas prices are inflated as a matter of course; and property values in the last couple of years have been rising by 15–20 per cent a year.

From an investment point of view, a holiday home in the Canaries will always yield a good return. It's the one place in Europe you can secure a rental income for the full twelve months of the year, October to March being the high season. Needless to say, though, there is a price to be paid – in this case not in money but in time. The flight from London to the Canaries is the wrong side of four hours, a tedious journey for any period less than a week. The Canary Islands are not the place for spontaneous weekend hops, but ideal for winter and summer holidays, and as a place for those thinking of retirement.

Tenerife

At 1231 square miles Tenerife is the largest island in the archipelago. It is also the most popular with the British, and has been for many years.

Dominating the whole island, from north coast to south and east to west, is the magnificent volcanic cone of Mount Teide. At 12,198 feet, its snow-capped peak is not only the highest point in Tenerife but the highest point on the whole of Spanish territory. Its towering presence is such that it forms its own weather pattern, and in turn forms two distinct areas on the island: north and south, as different from each other as black and white.

The Overseas Property Centre
YOUR INDEPENDENT PROPERTY CONSULTANTS

TENERIFE

COSTA BLANCA

MALLORCA

RETIREMENT

HOLIDAYS

INCOME

We publish property guides & monthly newsletters featuring special purchasing opportunities and legal safeguards.

Send for your copy today.

If you would like our independent advice and guidance on the type of property to purchase in the best location then please contact us. Advice on:- Tax, Offshore Companies, Rental, Building, Furnishing, Pensions, Medical, Schools, Insurance, Banking, Lawyers, Finance.

Hilton House
The Downs
Altrincham
Cheshire
WA14 2QD

Tel: 061-941 7022

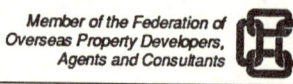

Member of the Federation of
Overseas Property Developers,
Agents and Consultants

The northern side of the island – fertile, humid and lush – is alive with exotic flowers, oranges, lemons, banana plantations and vineyards; tomatoes and geraniums grow like weeds by the roadside. The southern side, on the other hand, in the rain shadow of Mount Teide, is arid, barren and parched.

The south side of the island has only taken off since life-giving water was pumped over from the fertile side of the mountain in the 1970s, followed by the opening of its own airport at Reina Sofia in 1980. However, despite the south's growing popularity, British expatriates generally live in the north within a stone's throw of the capital, Santa Cruz, where they have been commercially established for two hundred years. With roots in shipping, bananas and wine, a colonial community lives on into the 1980s, with its own club and library, and even an Anglican church. The ever-present sunshine of the south is left for the holidaymakers.

Puerto de la Cruz, the leading tourist centre on the northern coast, has been home for a British community for a number of years. Today its popularity lives on, particularly among those looking for a retirement home. It is the centre for maritime and export traffic and offers plenty to amuse: hotels, restaurants, boutiques and bazaars. It doesn't pretend to compete with the sun, sea and sand resorts of the south, but for permanent living the climate is kinder; a few cloudy days, even some rain, can be a welcome break from month after month of sunshine.

Most of the properties in the area are bungalows or villas, built very much with the permanent resident in mind; some apartments are for sale as well. Many of the properties have spectacular clifftop views.

It is quite common for a house to be built to specification; the basic shell of a one-bedroomed bungalow can cost as little as £36,000; that of a two-bed bungalow, £40,000. These would have water and electricity, but no fitted kitchen, carpets or curtains. A comfortable resale villa suitable for permanent residence, with three bedrooms, fitted kitchen and bathroom, might cost anything from £80,000 depending on quality and location.

Puerto de la Cruz

1 bed apartment	£30,000–40,000
2 bed apartment	£35,000–45,000
1 bed bungalow	£45,000–70,000
2 bed bungalow/villa	£60,000–80,000
3 bed bungalow/villa	£80,000–100,000

In contrast to the north, the south is definitely nouveau. Children and teenagers prevail; discos and fast food are the order of the day. The main attraction is sunshine and long golden beaches (artificial, I'm afraid; left to nature they would be volcanic black).

Southern Tenerife must be one of the most extreme illustrations of man's impact on his environment. Only ten years ago, prior to the new airport and improved communications, it was little more than a desert of volcanic rock and ash, the last place you might consider for a holiday. Today, a scattering of developments stretches the length of the coast from El Medano to the giant Los Gigantes cliffs. Los Cristianos, once a quaint and tiny fishing village, now merges in a mass of hotels and apartment blocks with its neighbouring Playa de Las Americas. Las Americas, the prime winter resort on the island, didn't even exist then.

The volume market on Tenerife is now along this southern coast. It's the holidaymaker rather than the permanent resident whom the developers have in mind, and so most of the properties on the market are neat, easy-to-maintain apartments. Demand has pushed up prices, so they are now running at about 20 per cent above those in the north. A one-bedroom flat in Playa de Las Americas costs from around £35,000; a two-bedder from £50,000. If you have a villa in mind, a three-bedder with garden and pool costs upwards of £100,000. Any money spent, though, is well invested: a twelve-month rental season almost guarantees a 10 per cent net annual return.

Southern Tenerife

1 bed apartment	£35,000–50,000
2 bed apartment	£50,000–70,000
2–3 bed villa	£60,000–120,000
3–4 bed villa	£100,000–200,000

The 'golf colony' concept, so popular on mainland Spain and in Portugal, hasn't taken off to the same degree in Tenerife. There are just two on the island – Golf del Sur and the Amarilla Golf and Country Club – both within fifteen minutes' drive of the airport. Their emphasis is on leisure and sport in a completely self-contained environment. Central to both estates is the golf course and clubhouse, with tennis and squash courts necessary additions, as well as a marina in the case of the Amarilla Golf and Country Club. Commercial centres, restaurants and bars round off the package for owners of apartments, pueblos and villas on the estates. At Amarilla, properties range from one-bedroom apartments at £40,000 to three- and four-bedroom villas at between £140,000 and £180,000; a specially designed villa can cost up to £250,000. At Golf del Sur prices start at £31,000 for a studio, rising to upwards of £150,000 for a customized Canary-style villa with wood trimmings and low-pitched roof.

Country properties

Away from the coast, properties are progressively cheaper as you move further inland. Nine or ten miles inland, twenty minutes from the madding crowds of Playa de Las Americas, a deserted four- or five-roomed farmhouse costs between £35,000 and £45,000. An equivalent property in the hills can cost as little as £10,000 or £15,000.

A number of Canary Island *fincas*, long and low-lying, often L-shaped or U-shaped with a central courtyard and Moorish-tiled roofs, are dotted across the island. Almost all are in need of renovation. They were abandoned when, during the depression thirty to forty years ago, farmers simply upped and left to grow bananas in Venezuela, Argentina or Cuba. You might expect to pay £25,000–30,000 to bring a four- or five-roomed *finca* up to a comfortable living standard with new wiring, new roof and new floors. Installing water and electricity isn't usually a problem, providing the *finca* is near a village. The main worry is locating the owner, who by now has probably passed the property on to numerous children happily living in South America.

Country properties on Tenerife (approx. 10 miles inland)

	Unconverted	Cost to renovate
2–3 roomed farmhouse + 1–2 acres	£25,000–30,000	£20,000–25,000
4–5 roomed farmhouse + 1–2 acres	£35,000–45,000	£25,000–30,000
6–15 roomed farmhouse + 5 acres	£75,000–100,000	£50,000–60,000

Lanzarote

The most easterly of the Canary Islands, just sixty miles off the coast of Africa, Lanzarote is an island of striking scenery and extraordinary natural phenomena. As recently as the eighteenth and nineteenth centuries, great volcanic eruptions wiped out some 120 square miles and transformed the area into a mysterious lunar landscape, pockmarked with over three thousand volcanic cones and valleys of carbonized lava. In the south of the island, at La Montaña del Fuego, the charcoal-black ash still burns scorching hot just inches below the surface.

Left to nature, Lanzarote would be a desert. It is windy and very dry, and sometimes years go by without a single drop of rain, so there would be no greenery, no trees and no birdsong. As it is, water is seemingly squeezed out of stone to produce healthy crops of grapes, figs, melons, tomatoes and the famous Lanzarote onions. Protected by semi-circular stone walls, the plants thrive on night dew trapped in the volcanic ash.

On the coast, where high and low cliffs alternate with long stretches of beach, the islanders have created oases of palm trees and brightly coloured flowers. Clear waters and warm trade winds make for a windsurfer's paradise.

It's a relaxed place to spend a holiday. Life revolves around the sun, the sea and the nightlife. It's informal to the degree that a renowned property developer on the island recently attending a formal dinner in London had nothing to wear but a pair of faded jeans and a T-shirt.

Property developers are kept on a tight rein in Lanzarote. Although a few early planning mistakes were made, new development is tightly controlled. Except in the capital, Arrecife, anything above three storeys is banned; and on environmental grounds, as the law stands at the moment, no further land other than that already granted planning permission will be released for development. At the current rate of construction, this means that all building on the island will have been finished by 1991. Buildings have to be painted white, with woodwork painted green or left with the natural grain.

Puerto del Carmen

The international airport on the island is just outside Arrecife, the grimy, workaday commercial centre of the island. The majority of tourists, however, will bypass the capital altogether and head straight for Puerto del Carmen.

Situated on the most sheltered part of the island, conveniently close to the airport, Puerto del Carmen is the most developed resort on the island and the most commercialized. A wealth of restaurants, bars, shops and discos, and two golden beaches, satisfy the northern European demand. Prices, as a matter of course, have gone up in recent years, so that a good meal out now costs around £15 a head – expensive by Spanish standards.

Although Puerto del Carmen is geared largely for the tourist, there is a good selection of property for those intending to make a base there, whether for holidays or permanent residence. There are properties to suit all pockets: a small apartment, for example, on a large-scale development of a hundred or so units, or a four-bedroomed villa in its own grounds on the front line overlooking the ocean. The former could be picked up for around £25,000, the latter would set you back nearer £200,000. In between there are small apartment blocks, many with landscaped gardens and communal pool, and individual bungalows.

Puerto del Carmen

1 bed apartment	£25,000–35,000
2 bed apartment	£32,000–45,000
2 bed bungalow	£35,000–60,000
3 bed bungalow	£50,000–90,000
4 bed villa	£70,000–150,000

Playa Blanca

A decade ago, Playa Blanca was little more than a fishing village. Today it is one of the main development areas on the island. Situated in the far south, its main drawback is access. Either you hire a car or you catch the one bus a day from Arrecife. The town itself, with the old fishing village in the centre, has a number of bars, restaurants and clubs, although not in such abundance as in Puerto del Carmen. The attraction of the place is Papagayo Beach, a long, idyllic stretch of white sand approached only by a rough, unlaid road. In the absence of four-wheel drives, British, German and Scandinavian tourists (the Swedes have chosen this as their favoured resort) put their hired Pandas to the test to sun themselves on this popular beach.

The majority of freehold properties in Playa Blanca are bungalows, many on developments with gardens and a communal pool. Most popular are two-bedroomed bungalows suitable for holiday accommodation. A small bungalow can be picked up for as little as £40,000, although £50,000–60,000 is a more realistic figure. A villa in prime front-line position can cost upwards of £100,000.

Playa Blanca

2 bed bungalow	£50,000–75,000
3 bed bungalow	£60,000–100,000
4 bed bungalow/villa	£70,000–150,000

Costa Teguise

Just five minutes north of Arrecife, Costa Teguise is considered the most exclusive part of the island. It has no centre as such, just a scattering of low-density developments overlooking the ocean.

It was the brainchild of Union Explosivos Rio Tinto, one of Spain's largest multi-national companies. The company bought the land, put in the basic infrastructure including the all-important water desalination plant and a network of roads, built the five-star Las Salinas Sheraton hotel – and waited. Slowly the bidders came in.

Today, as well as a growing number of apartments and villas, it has shops, clubs, new restaurants opening all the time, the only golf course on the island (9-hole), and, of course, the beach. It is the breeziest and best beach for windsurfing on Lanzarote.

Property, whether apartment, bungalow or villa, tends to be a little more expensive in Costa Teguise than the other coastal developments.

Costa Teguise

1 bed apartment	£28,000–38,000
2 bed apartment	£38,000–50,000
2 bed bungalow	£50,000–80,000
3 bed bungalow/villa	£65,000–100,000
4 bed bungalow/villa	£75,000–150,000

Fuerteventura

One of the largest of the Canary Islands, Fuerteventura is comparable in size to Tenerife. Yet it has a tenth of the population, a fraction of the developments, and, unlike the other islands, mile after mile of white, sandy beach – blown, it is believed, from the Sahara Desert.

The south of the island, around Jandia, has been popular with German tourists for quite some time. However, the British have caught on to the delights of this largely unspoilt island in the last five or six years, gravitating mainly towards the fishing villages of Corralejo in the north-east and, more recently, Cotillo in the north-west. Both destinations are a short drive from the international airport just outside the capital, Puerto del Rosario. Alternatively you can fly to Lanzarote and take a forty-five-minute ferry ride.

Corralejo is the site of the only two hotels in the north of the island – Tres Islas and Oliva Beach Hotel. Planning controls are strict: residential developments must be low-density and low-rise – nothing more than two storeys. Most are geared towards the self-catering market – although, for the gourmet, there are several excellent and reasonably priced restaurants in town.

The main attraction of Corralejo is Oliva Beach, a long, idyllic stretch of pure white sand backed by magnificent rolling dunes. The beach is too big ever to be crowded, but to protect it from any such eventuality it has been designated a National Park. It's a marvellous playground for sunbathers, windsurfers and, most of all, divers. The stretch of water between Corralejo and the small island of Lobos is an underwater conservation area, offering some of the best scuba-diving in Europe.

Cotillo, on the west coast, is the new alternative coastal village to Corralejo. It has no dunes, but delightful sandy bays and calm lagoons. The village itself has an old harbour with a remarkably narrow entrance through which fishermen guide their boats on the crest of waves. It's less developed for the tourist than Cotillo, but nevertheless has a growing number of restaurants and bars.

Established developments, and those being developed around Corralejo and Cotillo, take the form of small apartment blocks and bungalows centred around manicured gardens and a swimming pool. There are rarely more than thirty units on a development, and as few as six or eight is common. Most are Moorish in style, painted white with low-pitched tiled roofs, arches, and balconies to make full use of the coastal views.

Fuerteventura

studio/1 bed apartment	£30,000–35,000
2 bed apartment	£45,000–60,000
semi-detached 2 bed 'chalet'	£65,000–85,000
2 bed bungalow	£60,000–90,000
3 bed villa	£90,000–125,000

An individual villa on the island might cost you upwards of £90,000. A luxury three-bedroomed villa, for instance, with a self-contained studio apartment, a garage and sea views across to Lobos and Lanzarote, would cost around £150,000.

Alternatively, you can buy a plot of land and build. The total cost of the plot and construction will obviously vary, depending on location and building specifications, but generally it can be assumed comparable in price to buying a ready-constructed villa of the same order. Around Corralejo and Cotillo there is no shortage of easy-to-manage plots of various sizes from around 2700 square feet. In *rustica* land, however, away from the coastline in the red hills of the interior, it is obligatory to buy at least 10,000 square metres (approximately 2½ acres), on which you can build only one dwelling on 30 per cent of the land.

Large-scale developments
Although property development on Fuerteventura is years behind that on Tenerife and Lanzarote, there is little doubt that it is gathering momentum. An indication of this is the large-scale developments now either undergoing construction or in the planning stages.

Parque Holandes, for instance, situated between Corralejo and Puerto del Rosario, comprises up-market chalets, maisonettes and villas on 140 acres of coastal land. The development already has a shopping precinct, restaurants and bars, and plans are underway to construct a sports complex, golf course, and, by 1992, a 400-berth marina.

Close to this development, a Swiss-backed company is investing some £200 million on a 62-acre project, Puerto Ventura. The plans here are to build yet another marina (supposedly the fourth largest in Europe), three hotels, two new beaches, plus a large number of apartments and villas.

Fuerteventura is undoubtedly finding its position on the tourist map. If planning controls are rigidly enforced, it should remain relatively unspoilt. However, not long ago there was only one direct flight a week to the island from Britain. Today there are five.

Buying and Selling

Spanish law applies – see pages 49–51.

CHAPTER 6
PORTUGAL

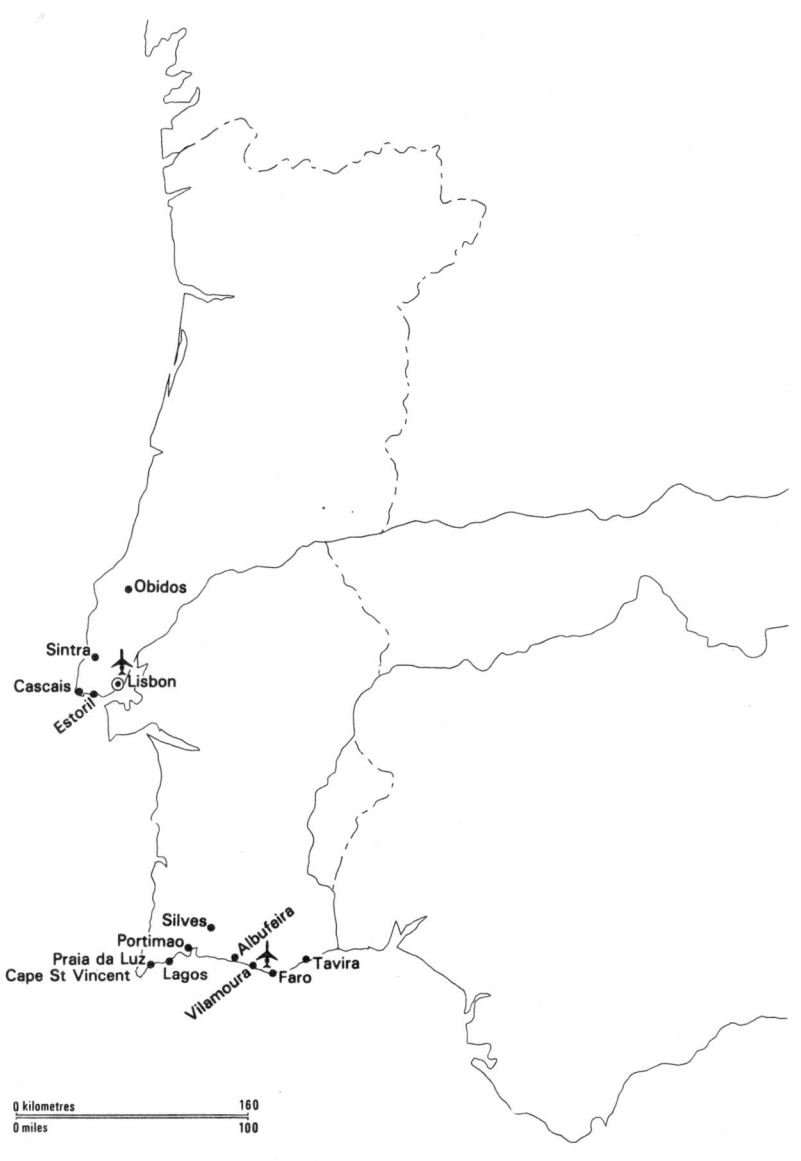

If anyone mourns the loss of the British Empire, they should spare a thought for Portugal, which was the first and one of the greatest colonial powers ever known. Inspired by Prince Henry the Navigator, the explorers Diaz, Vasco da Gama, Magellan and Cabral discovered and explored nearly two-thirds of the inhabited globe; Brazil, Angola, Mozambique and parts of India and the Far East were all included in the great Portuguese Empire.

Today the language lives on in memory. Two hundred million people around the world speak Portuguese, and yet Portugal is the poorest country in western Europe. Portugal's decline has been conclusive by any standards, yet despite this, and despite the political uncertainty following the bloodless coup of 1974 which marked the end of Portugal as a colonial power, there are signs afoot that Portugal might be coming back into its own. The election of the Social Democrats in 1985 signalled the end of a decade of political instability under numerous left-wing and socialist alliances. This, coupled with Portugal's entry into the European Community in 1986, has boosted confidence and encouraged foreign investment.

Perhaps because Portugal is one of the poorest countries in Europe, it has the most to benefit from joining the EC. New life is being injected into agriculture and the economy generally, and particularly into tourism. New motorways are planned, including one to link with a bridge over the River Guadiana into Spain.

This renewed confidence has been reflected in the property market. Prices on the Algarve and on the western coast around Estoril and Cascais have been rising steadily as a growing number of people, particularly the British, look to Portugal for a holiday home or place for retirement. The country has much to offer the foreign investor: it's just two and a half flying hours from London, the cost of living is low, the food is bountiful and fresh, the beaches washed clean by cool Atlantic waves; and on the Algarve, at least, there are numerous golf courses and over three thousand hours of sunshine a year.

The Algarve

Situated in the far south of Portugal, the Algarve offers nearly a hundred kilometres of sandy beaches, stretching from the Spanish border westwards to Cape St Vincent, the Land's End of western Europe. It is this south-facing coastline, sheltered from the Atlantic gales, that has attracted multitudes of sun-seeking tourists and property developers.

The name 'Algarve' originates from the Arabic *Al Garb*, meaning the west. The Moors dominated the region for five hundred years, and today their influence is still very much in evidence in the language, the music and the architecture; blue and white *azulejos* tiles, intricately decorated chimney pots and low, whitewashed houses are characteristic of this region, with many of the new developments adopting this traditional style.

Central Algarve

The first port of call for most tourists on the Algarve is Faro, the region's tiny capital and site of the international airport. Within twenty minutes' drive of Faro lie some of the most exclusive and most expensive country clubs and private estates in Portugal, if not in the whole of Europe. At Quinta do Lago, for instance, a 2000-acre estate of gentle, pine-clad hills, aptly named the Beverly Hills of the Algarve, a one-bedroomed apartment can cost upwards of £100,000. I visited a small villa complex within the estate where a three-bedroomed property now carrying a price tag of £210,000 had been sold for just £140,000 six months before, which shows the demand for such exclusivity. Here the wealthy mix with wealthy in private nightclubs, restaurants, bars and on the 27-hole championship golf course. It's a luxurious leisure estate that might be anywhere in the world. Only the timbered beach restaurants stuck far out on the dunes, serving exquisite and extraordinary fish, barbecued with garlic and served with fresh tomato salad, offer a hint that you might be on the Iberian peninsula.

It is in this central region of the Algarve, from Faro airport stretching west as far as Albufeira, that most of the holiday home developments are concentrated. Not all are as expansive as Quinta do Lago, but many have a golf course and associated clubhouse with swimming pool, bars and restaurant. Most offer a selection of apartments or individual villas, the prices of which vary with position – proximity to the golf course or the beach – and amenities offered. You could pick up a studio for around £40,000, or be the proud owner of a large villa with landscaped gardens and pool for £300,000. Generally, though, the price of properties on these purpose-built holiday developments falls into the categories in the table below.

Central Algarve

1 bed apartment	£40,000–65,000
2 bed apartment	£50,000–100,000
2 bed townhouse	£60,000–120,000
3 bed townhouse	£100,000–150,000
3–4 bed detached villa	£150,000–300,000

A slightly cheaper property might be found among the mix of small holiday developments that make up Vilamoura, a massive 4000-acre tourist 'urbanization' that has all but smothered the tiny fishing village of Quarteira. Vilamoura has two golf courses and a range of sporting facilities including tennis courts and stables, but the focus of Vilamoura is the thousand-berth marina with its boutiques, restaurants and bars. Construction is still taking place, but Vilamoura should eventually be able to accommodate and amuse fifty-five thousand holidaymakers at one sitting.

The western Algarve

Travelling west of Albufeira towards Cape St Vincent the scenery becomes hillier, more rugged and altogether more interesting. Property is a fraction of the price.

The western Algarve still offers a flavour of the traditional Portuguese way of life. The ancient town of Silves, once the Moorish capital of the Algarve, retains its old character and charm. There's the commercial port of Portimao with its harbour bustling with brightly bobbing fishing boats, and the favoured holiday resort of Lagos. Along this stretch of coastline deserted beaches can still be found, interspersed with tiny coves, rocky outcrops and grottoes.

So far this area west of Albufeira has been relatively unexploited, but development is taking place and will continue to do so as the road links from Faro improve. At Parque da Floresta, for instance, a development set in gentle rolling hills two hours drive from the airport, two- and three-bedroomed houses are being built in clusters around a golf course. The houses already completed have shown a 60 per cent increase in value in eighteen months and are now selling at between £90,000 and £110,000. One can only speculate that prices will continue to soar on completion of the bypass around Portimao. This should cut the travelling time from Faro by half.

Construction is also underway at the Waterside Village at Praia da Luz near Lagos. Designed to blend with the old village of Luz, Waterside Village includes a cluster of properties right by the beach, as well as a club with restaurants, bars, tennis courts and pools. New apartments are now being sold back from the front line on the beach for between £38,000 and £74,000.

Western Algarve

1 bed apartment	£30,000–40,000
2 bed apartment	£40,000–50,000
3 bed apartment	£50,000–80,000
3–4 bed detached villa	£100,000–150,000

The eastern Algarve

The eastern Algarve, stretching from Faro to the Spanish border, is one of the quietest and loveliest parts of Portugal. Watercolour scenes of long, sandy beaches and fertile plains carry the eye for mile upon mile to the gently rolling hills behind. It's tranquil and unspoilt, but for the tourist there are few facilities and not a golf course in sight – as yet. In time, the proposed motorway link over the River Guadiana into Spain might bring with it the holiday urbanizations and leisure facilities that seem never to fail to attract the Western tourist. But with luck, strict planning controls will ensure that construction doesn't destroy the natural beauty of this coastline.

Particularly attractive is the old regional capital, Tavira. The Venice of the Algarve, Tavira has fine seventeenth- and eighteenth-century squares and a delightful harbour, always buzzing with colour and activity. Property in the surrounding countryside is still cheap by Algarve standards, although prices have been rising quite steadily. A three-bedroomed villa, for instance, with breathtaking views across the plains and out to sea, costs between £70,000 and £100,000; a one-bedroomed apartment on the outskirts of town, around £30,000.

Eastern Algarve

1 bed apartment	£25,000–35,000
2 bed apartment	£35,000–50,000
3–4 bed villa	£70,000–100,000

Purpose-built developments are few and far between on the eastern Algarve. This makes the Marlin Country Club near Tavira quite an exception. Plans are that it will comprise seventy two-bedroomed townhouses priced between £45,000 and £70,000, plus swimming pool, tennis courts and restaurant.

The Estoril coast

Immediately to the west of Lisbon lies the Costa do Estoril, or the Costa do Sol, Portugal's sunshine Riviera where the Atlantic rollers sweep in tirelessly under breezy clear skies. It is also known as the Coast of Kings – its two famous resorts, Cascais and Estoril, were once the favoured leisure resorts of the Portuguese royal family, as well as a haven for exiled European royalty.

Today Estoril, with its casino and elegant hotels, and the old quarters of the fishing village of Cascais, retains the charm of former times; while the three golf courses in the area, tennis and squash courts and every form of watersport cater for the modern, fitness-conscious holidaymaker.

Property in the area isn't cheap. Largely dictated by the Lisbon market, the price of resale properties can easily match the most exclusive developments on the sunny Algarve. At Cascais, for example, a five-bedroomed villa with a garage and a quarter-acre of land can sell for upwards of £200,000. At Estoril, a three-bedroomed, three-bathroomed villa with small courtyard might cost £90,000 to £100,000; a less salubrious villa with three bedrooms, kitchen and pantry, £60,000. Prices vary enormously with size and position.

Few foreigners buy in Lisbon itself, unless they are there on business. Nevertheless, all kinds of properties at all kinds of prices can be found in this beautiful and historic city. At the top end of the market, a palatial villa with landscaped gardens, swimming pool and tennis court can cost upwards of a million pounds, as it might in any capital city, while on a more modest scale a small three-bedroomed villa could be found for nearer £60,000.

Long favoured by the British, the ancient hill town of Sintra, green and luxuriant even in summer, has a number of noble mansions and *quintas* (old farmhouses) well worth investigating. Examples include a four-bedroomed villa with self-contained annexe and swimming pool, price £279,000; or a newly built villa on a quarter-acre of land, price £60,000. A small two-bedroomed house, ancient and run-down but full of character, can be picked up for around £40,000.

Estoril, Cascais and Sintra

1 bed apartment	£25,000–40,000
2 bed apartment	£30,000–60,000
3 bed apartment	£35,000–70,000
2 bed villa	£55,000–80,000
3 bed villa	£70,000–150,000
4 bed villa	£90,000–200,000

The Silver Coast

Largely undiscovered by foreign visitors, the Silver Coast, some 50 miles north of Lisbon, offers mile after mile of deserted golden beach. It is an area where land and sea dominate the way of life, and many aspects of the rural scene have changed little over the years. Vineyards, market gardens, pine and eucalyptus plantations are only broken by enchanting historic towns and bustling fishing villages, and yet so far it has been protected from an invasion of tourists, largely because of the unpredictability of the Atlantic weather.

Nonetheless, there are a few developments on the market for those who don't mind the odd cloudy day shadowing their fortnight's break. Fifty miles from Lisbon airport, for instance, just four miles from the medieval walled town of Obidos, lies the Obidos Lagoon, an 800-acre nature reserve where tightly controlled development has been permitted to take place. A dividing sandbar ensures that the temperature of the lagoon is several degrees above that of the adjoining Atlantic.

To date a handful of apartments and two- and three-bedroomed townhouses overlooking the lagoon have been constructed. Prices range from £60,000 to £100,000. There are plans to put up a hotel with restaurant and pool, and a 27-hole golf course, but in the meantime the shallow, warm waters of the lagoon provide a natural playground for dinghy sailing and windsurfing, while the adventurous can venture across the sandbar to surf on the Atlantic waves.

Buying

When buying a property at home or abroad, it is advisable to employ a lawyer. Portugal is no exception. Whether you employ one in England or in Portugal doesn't matter; all that is important is that he has a specialist knowledge of Portuguese law.

If your chosen property is on a development, it is quite likely that you will be asked to sign an option or contract of reservation, and pay a small deposit of between £500 and £2000. Do so by all means, but check first that it is refundable if you decide not to go ahead.

At this stage, whether buying from a developer or an individual, you should make quite sure that the relevant searches are carried out on the property at the local land registry. Your lawyer should check that the vendor has good title to the land and that the property is not mortgaged, or subject to any other encumbrances. If the property is part of an estate or block of flats, a copy of the co-ownership rules and the latest accounts of the community of owners should be obtained. If it is still under construction, rigorous enquiries should be made to ensure that the developer is solvent and that his building programme is adequately funded.

The first legal document you will be asked to sign is a promissory contract of sale (*contracto de promessa de compa e vende*). Signed by both parties, this is a legally binding document stating at what time and what price the transfer will be completed. Usually you will be required to pay a 10 per cent deposit on signature, which is forfeited if for any reason you decide not to go ahead. If the vendor pulls out, he will be legally bound to pay you twice the sum of the deposit in compensation.

In order to comply with Portuguese exchange control regulations, the next stage is for your lawyer to apply for a licence from the Bank of Portugal for monies to be imported for the property purchase and furnishings. Funds must be in foreign currency, not in escudos.

Once the licence is issued, usually four to twenty weeks from the date of application, the title deed (*escritura*) can be transferred and the balance of funds paid over to the vendor. The transfer documents are drawn up by the notary of the municipality where the property is registered and signed by both vendor and purchaser, or by their representative powers of attorney. This transfer of deeds confers ownership of the property to the purchaser. However, until it is registered this can only be enforced against the vendor, and not against third parties. It is essential, then, to register ownership of the property at the local land registry without delay.

Needless to say, buying a property in Portugal involves paying taxes and fees. In Portugal these are carried wholly by the purchaser and usually amount to between 12 and 15 per cent of the purchase price. The bulk of the cost is the transfer tax (SISA), payable on a sliding scale up to 10 per cent of the value of the property or building plot. The maximum 10 per cent is payable on all properties valued at over 15 million escudos (approximately £60,000). Notary and registration fees amount to between 2 and 2½ per cent of the purchase price, on top of which you will have to pay solicitor's fees if you obtain independent legal advice.

Selling

If and when you come to sell a property in Portugal, you will face no problems repatriating the proceeds providing you have your original import licence proving that the necessary funds for purchase emanated from outside the country. Until recently, you would not have been charged capital gains tax on any profit made on the sale. However, the Portuguese government has now introduced capital gains tax on the sale of properties purchased after 1 January 1989. For the purpose of taxation, the capital gain becomes part of your income for the year in which it arises and is charged at half the relevant rate in the relevant tax band. If you sell a property but reinvest the gains in another property within two years, the capital gain will not be considered as chargeable income.

CHAPTER 7
GREECE

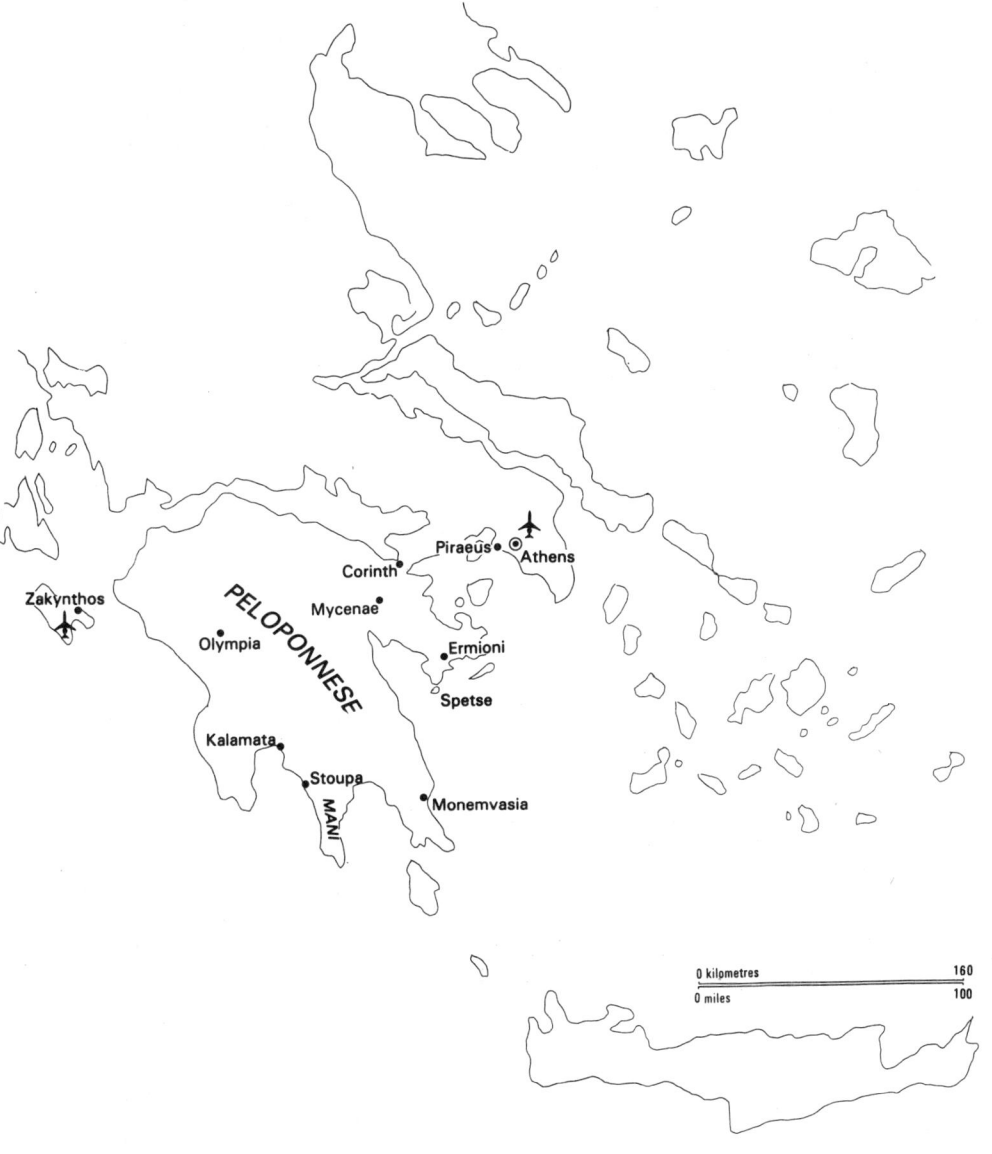

Many people are under the impression that it is not possible for foreigners to buy property in Greece. This is simply not true. The Greek government has always allowed the sale of freeholds to foreigners with the exception of certain islands and parts of the mainland close to neighbouring countries, designated as 'border areas' for reasons of national security. These prohibited areas happen to include some of the more popular tourist islands such as Crete, Corfu and Rhodes, but in time even these may be opened to the foreign investor. As a member of the EC, Greece is subject to European law which should permit a European citizen to buy anywhere within the Community. Meanwhile, there are still a multitude of Greek islands and attractive parts of the mainland to choose from.

Occupying the southern part of the Balkan peninsula, Greece has an extensive coastline and one of the best climates in the world in which to enjoy it. Here you get guaranteed sunshine from April to September. Taking into account the islands as well – the Ionian, Cyclades and Dodecanese – Greece is the perfect destination for sailing and water-sports of all descriptions.

While geared up for the holiday market, the country still manages to retain much of its traditional character and charm. Theatre, dance and festivals are an everyday event; the pace of life is relaxed, the people honest and friendly. Here, you can be secure in the knowledge that you will pay a fair price for a meal in a restaurant, and, what's more, your children will be welcomed at your table into the late evening hours. Children are the focus of Greek family life and adored by one and all. Although inflation has been running at about 20 per cent in Greece, the cost of living is still low relative to the United Kingdom, with the exception of electrical goods and cars. A good, if simple meal out with wine costs around £6 a head, and spirits are cheap if you stick to the local brands.

The British have been enjoying cheap and cheerful holidays in Greece for a number of years, but have never established a tradition of buying property there as they have in Spain or Portugal. A few pioneers have been investing in Greek property since the early part of the century, but generally the market for foreigners is still in its infancy. Among the Greeks themselves, the family home is traditionally handed down from one generation to the next, so that estate agents as we understand them are few and far between.

A few UK-based agents, however, do have Greek properties on their lists. These might be individual properties, or apartments in a small block of six or eight. There are only a handful of developments geared specifically at the foreign investor – the kind that offer a mix of apartments and villas and perhaps a communal garden and a swimming pool.

Despite the classical perfection of ancient Greek architecture, many of the modern buildings in Greece are poorly constructed with inadequate sanitation. The sight of iron girders protruding inelegantly from rooftops, just in case the owners decide to build another floor, is common. Quality is something to keep an eye on, although modern construction is improving all the time. Strict planning controls now ensure that modern development must be in keeping with the traditional architecture of the region. In Cyclades, for example, all new buildings must be flat-roofed and preferably feature the characteristic arches of the region; in the Peloponnese, buildings must be whitewashed or constructed from natural stone with traditional tiled roofs.

Peloponnese

South and west of Athens, the Peloponnese is separated from the mainland by a canal through the Isthmus of Corinth. Although strictly not an island, it has the feel of an island and the name of one. Peloponnese means the island of Pelops, the son of Tantalus on whom resistance to temptation was imposed.

Shaped like a mulberry leaf, the Peloponnese concentrates every geographical feature of Greece into just over 8000 square miles. It has rocky coasts and deserted, sandy beaches, barren hills, tree-clad mountains, and all the traditional Mediterranean crops: olives, vegetables and fruit, including grapes for wine and currants. It also has flourishing modern towns and old fishing villages, relics from ancient Greece and Byzantium, Frankish castles and historic monasteries at Olympia, Mycenae, Mani and Monemvasia. Most important, it is reasonably accessible from Athens. You can drive, catch the bus or hydrofoil. The hydrofoil to Ermioni, an attractive fishing village in one of the more developed parts of the Peloponnese, takes around three hours.

Most of the holiday properties can be found, naturally enough, around the coast. A one-bedroomed apartment in the Peloponnese can be picked up for around £25,000; a two-bed apartment, for £35,000. There are also small developments of terraced and detached villas, but not in great numbers. One that has been constructed specifically with the foreign investor in mind is at Stoupa, a small village on the south coast of the Peloponnese peninsula, clustered round two beautiful sandy bays. The development is in the centre of the village itself, in an olive grove, and offers one-, two- and three-bedroomed houses with fitted kitchens and bathrooms with baths (not just showers) for between £42,000 and £67,500. Stoupa is a long way from the main tourist centres, but can be reached either by bus or train from Athens, or by air from Athens to Kalamata airport, which is about an hour's drive away.

More conveniently situated at Ermioni and Corinth are a handful of developments comprising clusters of villas around a central swimming pool and clubhouse. Premiums are paid for this type of development, but generally the price of property in the Peloponnese falls into the brackets in the following table.

Peloponnese

1 bed apartment	£25,000–35,000
2 bed apartment	£30,000–45,000
2 bed villa	£40,000–55,000
3 bed villa	£65,000–100,000

The islands

Even discounting islands designated as 'border areas', the choice of islands on which to buy property in Greece is enormous. Santorini, Mykonos, Tinos and Paros are just a few in the Cyclades alone. There are enough islands to visit one a year for a lifetime, but when thoughts turn to buying property, one of the most important criteria is accessibility. The last thing you want is a day's ferry journey from Piraeus after fighting through the customs at Athens airport.

Zakynthos

One choice might be Zakynthos, an island a short distance off the north-western tip of the Peloponnese and the sixth largest of the Ionian islands. It has its own international airport with direct flights from the UK during the summer months, and domestic flights from Athens. It also has the usual ferry services that one might expect.

It's a popular island with the British, being unusually green for Greece, with low mountains covering a good deal of the interior. The beaches are golden sand and the water beautifully clear. Zakynthos town itself is a lively centre, rich in monuments, galleries, shops and tavernas.

Properties on Zakynthos are generally resale villas; there is virtually nothing built specifically for the holidaymaker. Villas can cost anything from £40,000–50,000 upwards. A small two-bedroomed house, for instance, about two miles from town and half a mile from the beach, costs around £40,000. This is a prefabricated structure and about as cheap as you will find, unless you are prepared to do some renovation work; if so you might pick up a small property, further inland, for between £25,000 and £30,000. Moving up the ladder, a newly constructed three-bedroomed house with an acre of land, close to the beach, costs around £110,000. Although the cost of living in Greece is cheap, the price of properties needn't be.

Zakynthos

2 bed villa	£40,000–60,000
3 bed villa	£50,000–80,000
4 bed villa	£90,000–150,000

Spetse

Another popular choice is Spetse. The most southerly of the Saronic Gulf islands, it lies just a mile and a bit off the Argolid peninsula. Tiny red and white water taxis buzz back and forth from the mainland to the island's Dapia harbour with scenic regularity.

Although popular with the Athenians for summer weekend breaks, Spetse is rarely too crowded and yet, out of season, still bustles with local activity. Here the locals build boats and collect the resin used in the making of retsina, the local Greek wine. Sweet-smelling pine trees cover much of the island.

Spetsai town itself brims with restaurants, tavernas and shops. Elegant nineteenth-century mansions line the waterfront, and, dotted through the town's narrow cobbled alleyways, designs of mythical marine figures made from different-coloured pebbles decorate the buildings. The charm of the place is enhanced by the fact that motor vehicles are not allowed on the island.

The occasional resale property comes up for sale on the island, but because of their scarcity they tend to command very high prices. A small two- or three-bedroomed property in need of substantial renovation, for instance, can cost between £30,000 and £45,000. A renovated three- or four-bedroomed villa can cost anything from £130,000 upwards.

In the last year or two a small number of developments geared specifically at the overseas investor have also come on to the market. In Spetsai town, for instance, elevated on high land overlooking the harbour, a mix of apartments and townhouses are selling for between £32,000 and £91,000. They are of traditional style, painted white, with balconies and low-pitched, red-tiled roofs. In Baltisa, a quieter part of the island away from the tourist spots, there is a complex of one-, two- and three-bedroomed apartments in eight separate villas, again painted white with red-tiled roofs; these sell for between £16,000 and £80,000. The estate is just two minutes' walk from a marina.

Holiday properties on Spetse

studio apartment	£16,000–18,000
1 bed apartment	£20,000–40,000
2 bed apartment	£59,000–85,000
2–3 bed townhouse	£80,000–90,000

Resale villas on Spetse

2 bed villa	£45,000–60,000
3–4 bed villa	£130,000–250,000

An island of your own

Another wild and wonderful option in Greece is to join the Onassises and Rothschilds of this world and buy an island of your own. The idea isn't as outrageous as you might expect when you look at the price tags of islands in Greek waters that have recently been on the market. A pair of islands about twenty minutes' boat ride from the mainland were recently on the market for US$75,000 each. They were small, about 2½ and 7½ acres, covered with bushes and trees and, according to the locals, had no water supply of their own. Nevertheless, they provided ample space on which to build and would have made idyllic island retreats from which to sail and entertain your friends as you pleased.

Country properties

Old farmhouses of suitable character and size for conversion are few and far between on the Greek islands and mainland. There are, however, a few old merchants and tradesmen's houses to be found, mainly on the Peloponnese.

After 'negotiation', you can expect to pay between £30,000 and £40,000 for an old two-bedroomed property in need of tender loving care. A larger, two-storey property with perhaps three or four bedrooms might cost between £50,000 and £70,000. Often these properties will belong to several members of a family; it is essential to clear the title before purchase.

Maintenance, repairs and new building

Organizing maintenance and repairs in Greece isn't as easy as it might be. A telephone can take up to a year to install, as can water and electricity.

If you are considering building your own house and you don't have contacts in Greece, it is strongly recommended that you hand all responsibility over to a developer who can be on the spot at all times. Tackled this way, it is quite possible to put up a three-bedroomed property on the Peloponnese with, say, a quarter of an acre of land, for around £50,000. The governing factor is the cost of land. On some of the islands, say Paros or Skiathos, the price could be £60,000 or less. On Mikonos, where land is in short supply, it could be as much as £80,000–90,000.

Buying

Until recently, few British buyers were interested because historically it has not been possible to repatriate money taken into Greece to buy property. Now, with the entry of Greece into the European Community, all that has changed. The subsequent lifting of currency restrictions allows a foreigner to repatriate not only the original sum taken into Greece, but also any additional money accrued through reasonable appreciation of the property on resale.

With the exception of the 'border areas' already mentioned, a foreign national is equal to a Greek national from the standpoint of legal protection from the moment that he has actually bought a property in Greece.

All property in Greece is freehold, and having found one to suit your needs, the first step is to employ a Greek lawyer to carry out the necessary searches to ensure that there is no legal lien or dispute of a third party over the property. All going well, a sales contract is drafted by a notary public in the presence of both vendor and purchaser and their respective lawyers.

Before execution of the contract, the local inland revenue authority will assess the sum of the property transfer tax to be paid. This tax is similar to our stamp duty in the United Kingdom, although it will make a far bigger hole in your pocket than the UK equivalent. Property transfer tax in Greece is 9 per cent of any purchase price up to 4 million drachmas (approximately £15,000), and 11 per cent thereafter. In addition, there is a 3 per cent local community charge to be paid on the net amount of the property transfer tax as calculated. For example, in the case of a house sold for 6 million drachmas, the transfer tax payable is 4 million drachmas × 9 per cent + 2 million drachmas × 11 per cent = 580,000 drachmas. The local community tax is an additional 580,000 drachmas × 3 per cent = 17,400 drachmas.

Once this payment is out of the way, completion of the transaction can take place. The sales contract is signed by both vendor and purchaser, or, if they are unable to be present, through proxies. It is quite usual to grant power of attorney to your lawyer.

If neither vendor nor purchaser is a Greek national, the transaction may be completed before any Greek consul abroad – convenient if you buy a Greek property from a British owner. In this case the purchase price can be paid in foreign currency outside Greece, without any obligation on the vendor's part to collect the proceeds in Greece either in foreign currency or in drachmas.

If the vendor is Greek, however, the transaction must take place in Greece before a notary public. As the purchaser, you must ensure that the necessary funds for purchase of the property and payment of the transfer tax are imported from outside Greece through normal banking channels. It is essential, at this stage, that express and specific indication is made on the relevant transfer statements that the funds are to be used for the purchase of a specific property at a specific address. Following importation, the funds will be converted into drachmas and you will be issued with a conversion slip, known as a pink slip.

The final stage is for the notary to register the transfer deeds with the appropriate land registry and for you to pay him his fees. Notarial charges are typically 2½ per cent of the purchase price, while in addition there is a compulsory contribution of approximately 1 per cent of the purchase price to be paid to the local law society.

Selling

If and when you come to sell a property in Greece, you will be able to repatriate a sum equivalent to the original imported funds plus any money accrued through reasonable appreciation, providing you can produce your pink slip proving that the necessary funds for the purchase originated from outside Greece. There is no capital gains tax on profits made from the resale.

CHAPTER 8
CYPRUS

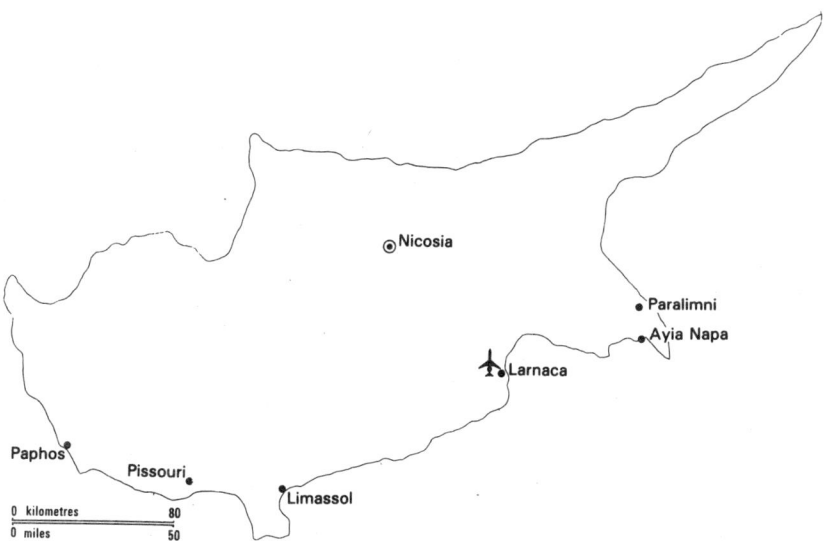

There is something about this island of Aphrodite that draws visitors back and back again. It is beautiful, but not the most beautiful of Mediterranean islands; it is hot, but so are a lot of places; it has only one golf course and no horse-racing, and yet the British like it. Its attractiveness lies in its people. In Cyprus the word *xenos*, stranger, also means guest. For Cypriots hospitality is something sacred, and to this day this feeling envelops any visitor to the island.

British people, in particular, feel welcome in Cyprus – not surprisingly, since the island was governed by the British from 1878 until it became independent in 1960. English is written, spoken and widely understood by almost everyone. Street signs are familiar, and the Cypriots drive on the left-hand side of the road. The legal system is still based on Britain's, and the two British army bases at Episkopi and Dekelia are still sovereign UK territory. The island even has two branches of Marks and Spencers.

All this Britishness, yet the island is set in the eastern Mediterranean at the crossroads of Europe, Asia and Africa. Cyprus has 340 days of sunshine a year and a sea temperature that never drops below 60°F even in January; in high summer it reaches near-bathwater temperature at 90°F. The landscape is dry and arid, broken only by olive trees and vineyards and the occasional burst of colour from flowering bougainvillea and hibiscus. Its coastline is rugged in places, interspersed with long, sandy beaches, while its interior is mountainous. The Troodos mountain range, covered with scented forests of cedar and pine, stretches the breadth of the southern half of the island.

The north of the island has been occupied by the Turkish army since 1974. The capital, Nicosia, roughly in the centre of the island, is divided physically, like Berlin, into two; the so-called 'green line' separates the Greek Cypriots in the south from the Turkish Cypriots in the north. The northern area has the best beaches and had the greatest concentration of holiday and tourist developments, but since the occupation tourism has moved with the Greek Cypriot refugees to the more heavily industrialized south. A new airport was built at Larnaca in the south-east, and later another at Paphos in the south-west, to cater for the growing number of tourists visiting this part of the island.

The flight to Cyprus from the UK takes four and a half hours and is expensive by inter-European standards, but once you arrive you are warmly received. Around two thousand Britons choose to live permanently in Cyprus and several thousand more own holiday homes on the island – for several reasons. Apart from the common use of the English language and the hospitality and honesty of the people – crime is virtually unheard of on the island – property is relatively inexpensive and the cost of living is around the cheapest in Europe. A good, if simple meal out for two costs between C£8 and C£12 (between about £9 and £15 sterling). Cigarettes cost the equivalent of about 60p a packet, and a good bottle of Cypriot wine about £1.20. Rates are lower, as are gas and electricity bills. And in addition there are very favourable tax concessions, particularly for retired people living on the island.

The cost of property varies depending on the facilities offered and proximity to the beach, but generally prices on the whole of the island fall into the following brackets:

Cyprus

1 bed apartment	£20,000–25,000
2 bed apartment	£26,000–36,000
2 bed terraced villa	£34,000–38,000
3 bed terraced villa	£42,000–48,000
2 bed detached villa	£40,000–80,000
3 bed detached villa	£65,000–170,000

Paphos

'Scratch the soil anywhere in Cyprus,' they say, 'and you will find traces of its magnificent past.' Nowhere is this more true than in Paphos. Designated a World Heritage town by the United Nations, Paphos is famed for its ancient Greek and Roman remains, including some of the finest mosaics to be found in the Mediterranean at the houses of Dionysos and Theseus.

Until 1974 Paphos was a picturesque but unexplored fishing village, quietly harbouring these wonderful treasures. In the last ten years or so, tourism has brought with it hotels and holiday home developments, aimed mainly at the foreign investor. However, despite rapid growth, Paphos, more than anywhere on the island, has kept a close rein on development. There are no high-rise buildings to speak of, most being no more than two storeys high. Construction on sites of historical importance is prohibited, and building density kept to a minimum.

For a British investor considering a holiday home or place for retirement in Cyprus, Paphos is a natural choice. It has a number of cheap and cheerful fish restaurants along its harbour front, a hospital and Anglo–American school, all the banking and financial services you might need, and some of the best beaches in the area. It also has its own international airport, opened in 1984.

A small one-bedroom flat can still be picked up in Paphos for as little as £20,000, a two-bedroom flat for around £26,000. A number of the properties are built in clusters around a central pool, often with communal gardens and perhaps a clubhouse and sports facilities. A three-bedroomed maisonette or terraced villa in one of these developments might cost between £42,000 and £48,000; a detached villa, anything from £68,000 up to £170,000.

Up in the foothills of the Troodos mountains, about six miles from Paphos, is the newly built Kamares village. Covering 250 acres of high land overlooking the coastal plains and Paphos Bay, this is the largest development on the island. Kamares means arches, and there are plenty of these in evidence in the architectural design of the villas on the estate. All are detached, and many have terraced gardens and private swimming pools. Prices start at around £50,000 for a two-bedroomed bungalow, rising to £250,000. The village also has its own clubhouse with swimming pool, tennis courts and restaurant for the residents. At 900 feet above sea level, it does not suffer the humidity of high summer and makes a good choice for permanent residence.

Larnaca and Limassol

Situated on the south-east coast, Larnaca was the chosen site for the first new international airport after the occupation of the northern territory. Previously a small industrial town, it is now something of a holiday resort. Hotels stretch the length of the beach; it has a new harbour and a marina, and numerous tavernas and cafés along the seafront. Apartment blocks make up the majority of holiday accommodation on the market.

About an hour's drive west along the coast is Limassol, the main commercial port of Cyprus and a bustling tourist resort. Since 1974 the beach frontage and number of buildings in Limassol has doubled. Modern hotels, holiday apartments, tavernas, discos and nightclubs stretch for miles along the seafront. It's a cheerful, cosmopolitan holiday spot, while at the same time retaining its workaday character.

The selection of property available in Limassol ranges from apartments through bungalows to smart detached villas in complexes with pools, tennis courts, restaurants and shops. One or two developments offer free membership to neighbouring hotels.

Pissouri village

Twenty-two miles west of Limassol, and just fifteen miles from the new airport at Paphos, is Pissouri village. Perched high on the hill overlooking the sea, Pissouri retains much of its old Cypriot charm. Tourism is new in these parts and in the village's fine old square, lined with mulberry trees and tavernas, the locals still spend endless hours sipping ouzo and sharing gossip.

Between the old village and the beach, a new development named after the village offers a choice of two- and three-bedroomed terraced and detached villas selling at prices from £38,000. A short drive from the estate takes you through vineyards to a long, sandy beach.

Ayia Napa and Paralimni

Some 20 miles east of Larnaca, this area is famed for its long, silvery beaches and turquoise waters. Life revolves around the sun and the sea. It's a paradise for watersports of all descriptions, while with a boat or a four-wheel drive it is still possible to find a deserted cove away from it all. Long favoured by the Scandinavians, this area is now gaining popularity with the British.

The villages of Ayia Napa and Paralimni themselves are inland, but along the coast modern hotels and aparthotels have sprung up to cater purely for the tourist trade. In the summer these are buzzing, but life comes and goes with the holidaymakers and in the winter they are dead. Most of the developments are geared for holiday use. There are apartments and a few villa developments with maybe ten or twelve properties grouped around a central pool.

At night, sunburnt bodies head for the hotel bars or to one of the villages. Ayia Napa in particular caters well for the visitor, with wine bars, nightclubs, bouzouki clubs and discos. In the winter months, the locals are left alone to engage in their traditional pastime of farming. Potatoes, tomatoes, beans and cucumbers grow well in the surrounding fertile land. Dotted across the landscape, windmills glint prettily in the sunshine as they draw water from deep beneath the soil.

Country properties

The British have always had a thing about buying anything old and with character that needs a bit of DIY. There was a time when you could buy an ancient Cypriot cottage with a few orange and lemon trees in the garden for next to nothing, but now cottages of character are relatively expensive and, together with the bill for repairs, may cost more than a new villa of an equivalent size. Often renovation involves completely rebuilding a property around a couple of original walls of stone or even mud bricks.

The best approach is to visit the village of your choice and ask for the village *muchtar*, the chairman of the local parish. He will probably be of more help than an estate agent. It is important to find a property with clear deeds – often several members of a family have stakes in a single property – and to obtain a firm estimate for any repair work before entering into a sales contract. Prices vary enormously with the popularity of the village, the amount of land and supply of water and electricity. You should budget between £10,000 and £40,000 for a rural wreck, although all prices are subject to 'negotiation'.

Country properties

2 bed country house, converted	£25,000–45,000
3 bed country house, converted	£35,000–60,000
4–5 bed country house, converted	£45,000–120,000

Buying

The word 'alien' comes up a good deal in the legal jargon relating to property acquisition in Cyprus. Don't be perturbed – it isn't an unfriendly reference to beings from another planet, but rather a straightforward term used to define any person who is not a citizen of the Republic. You and I are 'aliens', but welcomed in Cyprus with open arms – providing we stick to the rules.

The first rule concerns the size and type of property that non-Cypriots are allowed to buy. Aliens are limited to the purchase of one apartment, one house or one plot of land not exceeding two donums – about two-thirds of an acre.

Secondly, all aliens intending to register a property in Cyprus must apply for permission from the Council of Ministers. Permission is granted in all bona fide cases provided that the property is not intended for commercial exploitation. Strictly speaking, this means that it is illegal to buy a property to rent out for profit.

Thirdly, to satisfy exchange control regulations funds for purchasing a property should be transferred from outside Cyprus through an authorized commercial bank. When a property is transferred to the name of the alien, proof of importation of funds should be presented to the district land registry office before the registration is effected.

Before entering into a contract it is essential to carry out the necessary searches at the district lands' office. Your lawyer should check whether the property is encumbered in any way, and whether there is already a title deed in the name of the seller. If there is not, he should check whether the issue of such a title deed is legally feasible. Do not enter into a contract before being assured by your lawyer that the case is one in which the relevant permissions from the authorities would, as a rule, be granted.

When entering into a contract, make quite sure that there are ample and proper provisions ensuring that the contract is subject to obtaining the relevant permissions from the authorities, and, in the case of a flat, that there are conditions attached to the contract binding the rights and obligations of all other purchasers of flats in the same building.

The contract should be signed by both vendor and purchaser in the presence of two authorized witnesses. Power of attorney may be granted in the case of absence.

The next stage, to be carried out as soon as practicable, is to put in an application for permission from the Council of Ministers and an application to the Central Bank of Cyprus for an exchange control permit. As soon as these are obtained, the transfer of ownership can be completed by a simple process of registration with the district lands' office.

During the course of the registration procedure the value of the property will be reviewed by the district lands' office valuers for the purpose of determining the amount of transfer fees payable. The valuers may or may not accept the purchase value stipulated in the sales contract. Transfer fees are charged on a sliding scale from 5 per cent on the first C£10,000 up to 8 per cent on any amount over C£75,000. There is also stamp duty payable at C£1.50 per C£1000 to the value of C£100,000 and C£2 per C£1000 thereafter.

Selling

If and when you come to selling a property in Cyprus, you will not have to pay any capital gains tax. However, you will only be able to take out of the country the original sum used to purchase the property. Any profit should be placed in a blocked account with a commercial bank in Cyprus from which it can be repatriated at the rate of C£5000 per annum, plus interest earned during the year.

A non-resident selling a property to another non-resident on the basis of an agreement concluded outside Cyprus may receive the entire proceeds abroad without prior exchange control permit. In such circumstances, however, the new non-resident owner will not, on disposal of the property, have the right of release of an amount equal to the original cost. Instead, the entire proceeds from the sale must be placed in a blocked account and released at the rate of C£5000 a year plus interest.

CHAPTER 9
TURKEY

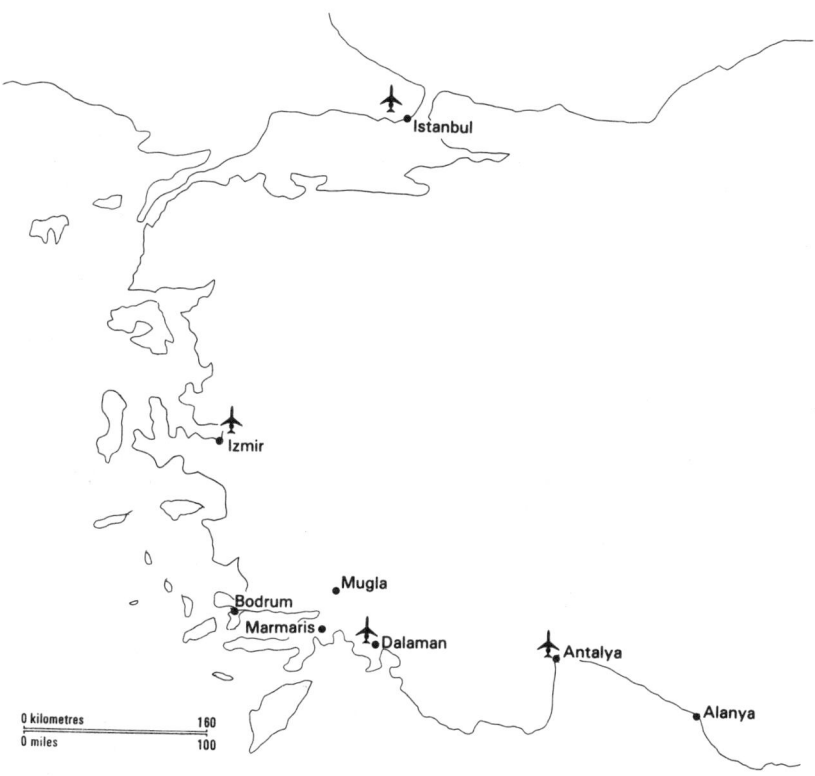

This is the one country people say you should visit now before its ancient sites and rich geography are ruined in the same way as those of its neighbouring Mediterranean hot spots. However, judging by the increase in the number of tourists visiting each year, the romantics seeking dreamy fishing villages and deserted beaches might discover that they have already missed the boat. Over 3.3 million tourists, many of them British, explored this new holiday destination in 1988, compared with just 2.3 million the year before. Inevitably the Turkish holiday home market will follow in the footsteps of the country's fast-developing tourist industry.

Turkey's problem, despite the recent growth in its tourist industry, is that it is still years behind other Mediterranean countries in terms of income generated from tourism. It desperately wants to catch up, but at the same time it doesn't want to destroy its sweeping bays and unpolluted waters that attracted the tourists in the first place.

The Turkish government has zoned large stretches of its Aegean and Mediterranean coast, from Izmir in the north, south through Bodrum and east through Marmaris to Antalya, as prime tourist development areas. Marmaris, once a small harbour town encircled by pine-covered hills, now sprawls in a mass of shoebox hotels and apartment blocks of varying quality and varying stages of development – hardly a recipe for a holiday paradise.

Fortunately, though, attempts are now being made to restrain unscrupulous developers. Planning controls are being tightened up, and generally the trend is towards low-density, low-rise buildings, constructed in sympathy with the local architecture. In Bodrum, for example, a seaside resort popular with the Turks as well as the British, all new developments must be flat-roofed with balconies and painted white.

Although ongoing development is all too apparent in many of the resorts on the Aegean and Mediterranean coasts, the scope for foreign property buyers is limited. British developers, encouraged by various tax incentives and forms of deferred payment, are slowly moving in, but in the main the properties are Turkish-built and poorly advertised to foreigners.

Foreign property purchase in Turkey is so new that the rules and regulations have not been firmly established. It is not a country for the timid investor. Having said that, Turkey is keen to join the Common Market and is unlikely to stir up problems for the European property buyer. It is the adventurous who often make the biggest returns in the long run.

Those who do take the plunge will still be able to find, if they look away from the main tourist resorts, a coastline little different from that of southern Spain before the mass development of the 1960s transformed it beyond recognition. They will also discover a wealth of treasures left by successive civilizations – Greek, Roman, Byzantine, Crusader and Ottoman – strewn across the countryside.

The cost of living is low by British standards, mainly due to rampant inflation (officially 30 per cent, unofficially much higher) and a weak Turkish lira. Taxis, buses and local products such as leather, jewellery, carpets and Turkish delight are all inexpensive. Food is also reasonably priced, and often excellent. Typically, local restaurants will serve an array of *meze* – hot and cold starters, including hundreds of variations of aubergine and local yoghurt – followed by a choice of lamb or fish, often cooked in garlic and oil and garnished with herbs. In many of the tourist resorts the price paid for cheap living is in the form of rough, dusty roads, primitive sanitation and electricity, and water that tends to come and go as it pleases, although the newer property developments usually manage to overcome these problems.

Flights from London to Turkey take around four hours and are more expensive from November to March. Cheap charter flights are available in the summer months. You can fly direct to Istanbul, or, for the Aegean and Mediterranean coasts, to Izmir, Dalaman or Antalya.

Turkish Properties & Rentals Ltd

THE FIRST ESTATE AGENT OUTSIDE TURKEY SPECIALISING EXCLUSIVELY IN TURKISH PROPERTIES

- Sales of residential/commercial property and land.
- Free advice on legal aspects of purchasing real-estate in Turkey.
- Representative offices in Turkey.
- Inspection visits.
- Property search service for individual requirements.
- Complete decoration of the properties through our factory.
- Property management service for our clients.
- Holiday rentals of villas and apartments.
- Flights at competitive rates.
- Car hire service.
- Constructors of a unique villa development in southern Turkey to be on the market in summer 1991.

57 GROSVENOR STREET,
MAYFAIR,
LONDON W1X 9DA
TEL: 01-355 4068 — 01-629 9544
TELEX: 23515 BRFM G — FAX: 01-629 2057

Bodrum

Just across the water from the Greek island of Cos, Bodrum, the ancient Halicarnassus, is today one of Turkey's most prominent international resorts on the Aegean coast. Its picturesque harbour, bordered by white villas and palm trees, is dominated by the magnificent medieval Castle of St Peter, just one of the town's many historical riches including the Tomb of Mausolus, one of the seven wonders of the ancient world.

Today its main attractions, though, are its cafés and bars, its sailing facilities and its bazaar, a colourful event held twice a week. It has a disco, aptly named the Halicarnassus, that is built in the shape of an amphitheatre and attracts hundreds of holidaymakers every night to dance in its open-air marbled splendour.

The drawback of Bodrum is that its beaches are narrow and shingly; the only options are to swim from the wooden jetties or catch a bus or boat out of town to one of the neighbouring unexplored and often deserted bays. Another disadvantage is that Bodrum is a good three or four hours' drive from Izmir airport, or two hours' drive from Dalaman airport. By the early 1990s, however, a new international airport should be up and running at Muğla, less than an hour's drive from Bodrum.

In Bodrum itself, as in any Turkish town, it is almost impossible to give specific prices for one-off individual properties. The idea of Turks outside the property business selling to foreigners is hardly even in its infancy; besides which, any price is likely to be settled 'by negotiation'. There are, however, small apartment blocks and small villa complexes with perhaps six or eight villas on the market. For example, three self-contained, two-bedroomed flats in a detached villa with a garden, a mile from Bodrum town, were priced at £23,000 each; and at a complex of eight two-bedroomed villas with balconies and garden close to the centre of town, the price quoted was £26,000 per villa.

Bodrum

2 bed apartment	£17,000–25,000
3 bed apartment	£20,000–32,000
2 bed villa	£25,000–40,000
3 bed villa	£30,000–60,000

In the countryside surrounding Bodrum, often in idyllic settings overlooking untouched inlets and bays, a small number of more sophisticated developments are emerging from the dust, in a few cases with British money involved. Developments with swimming pools, tennis courts, shops with commercial centres, restaurants, medical centres, and telex and fax – all the essentials for today's discerning holiday home buyer – are still few and far between. However, the trend towards this quality of development seems likely to follow that in Spain and Portugal. Most of these new properties in Turkey are villas, or villas split top and bottom into two apartments, with fitted kitchens and bathrooms and marble finish. The prices, not surprisingly, are higher than those of average Turkish properties.

Better-quality developments outside Bodrum

2 bed apartment	£25,000–35,000
3 bed apartment	£35,000–45,000
3–4 bed villa	£45,000–100,000

Marmaris

On a peninsula south of Bodrum, at the confluence of the Aegean and the Mediterranean, Marmaris sits at the head of a bay in a deep and sheltered inlet. It was once a small town with a few hotels established around the beach, but its pretty red-roofed houses are now overshadowed by a strip several miles long of new hotels and holiday villages, many of them yet to be completed. Marmaris is expanding to cater for the growing number of tourists visiting each year. For those seeking refuge, an endless stream of boats carries visitors to peaceful neighbouring shores backed by pine-clad hills.

In Marmaris, as in Bodrum, there is a choice of small apartment blocks and small villa complexes. A new building, for instance, overlooking the bay, might comprise twenty two-bedroomed apartments ranging in price from £25,000 to £34,000. A new three-bedroomed villa in a small complex costs around £45,000. Prices vary, of course, with quality and location, but in general tend to be a little more expensive than in Bodrum.

Marmaris

2 bed apartment	£23,000–40,000
3 bed apartment	£30,000–60,000
2 bed villa	£27,000–42,000
3 bed villa	£35,000–70,000

Mediterranean coast

Mark Anthony once gave part of Turkey's southern Mediterranean shores to Cleopatra as a wedding gift. Its sandy coves, translucent waters and forests of palm and pine befit such a present.

The principal resort of the region is Antalya, perched on the cliffs of a wide, crescent-shaped bay surrounded by the Toros mountains. It's an attractive port of call with shady, palm-lined boulevards, picturesque old quarters and a lively harbour. For the holiday home market, though, the best bet is Alanya, 80 miles east of Antalya and about two hours' drive from the airport.

Alanya is purpose-built for the tourist. It has long white beaches, modern motels, hotels and countless fish restaurants and cafés along the seafront. It is perfect for sunbathing and watersports of all descriptions. It also has a delightful old town with a harbour famous for its extraordinary arched boatyards built by the Seljuks, who ruled Turkey in the Middle Ages before the Ottomans took over; and, dominating the town, old and new, a Seljuk fortress jutting out on a rock promontory 850 feet above sea level.

Holiday accommodation in Alanya can be picked up for surprisingly little money. A small one-bedroomed flat, perhaps ten years old, can cost as little £12,000; a two-bedroomed flat in a five-storey block, back from the seafront, around £15,000. A villa with three bedrooms and a small garden, 250 yards from the beach, might cost around £23,000.

Mediterranean coast

1 bed flat	£12,000–15,000
2 bed flat	£14,000–18,000
3 bed flat	£17,000–25,000
3 bed villa	£20,000–30,000

Istanbul

It is impossible to write a chapter on Turkey without at least a brief mention of Istanbul, its magnificent capital city straddling Europe and Asia. Once the capital of two great empires – Byzantine and Ottoman – this city of minarets rising either side of the Bosphoros offers the pleasures of both east and west.

The market for British property buyers in Istanbul is only just opening up, and is more likely to appeal to the businessman or very wealthy individual. From Istanbul you can take a helicopter to the ski slopes at Uludag in winter, and sail in the Sea of Marmara and the Black Sea in the summer.

On both the European and Asian side of the Bosphoros there is a small selection of prestigious developments on the market with magnificent views, shopping facilities, restaurants, communal sports centres, tennis courts, swimming pools and even helicopter landing pads. Something quite new to Turkey is the golfing estate: this is arriving in the form of a joint British–Turkish venture in a green belt area twenty-five minutes' drive out of town. Top-of-the-range, fully fitted villas with private swimming pools can top £600,000 on one of these up-market developments.

The price of these luxurious properties far and away exceeds the price of individual resale properties in the centre of town. Prices tend to fluctuate with the state of the economy, but generally speaking a two-bedroomed flat in a good area can be found for around £50,000; and a reasonable three- or four- bedroomed apartment for between £70,000 and £120,000. A large family villa in a desirable residential area might cost £200,000. For those considering a studio or one-bedroomed apartment, they are virtually unheard of in Istanbul.

Istanbul

2 bed apartment	£40,000–120,000
3 bed apartment	£60,000–150,000
4 bed apartment	£80,000–180,000
3 bed villa	£100,000–200,000
4 bed villa	£120,000–250,000

Buying

The concept of foreigners buying property in Turkey is so new that even Turkish lawyers admit to having difficulties in keeping up with the changing regulations and laws. The restrictions and procedures involved in buying a home in Turkey outlined below should therefore only be taken as a guide. If and when you decide to buy a property in Turkey, you are recommended to obtain advice from the British Consulate in your chosen area of purchase, as well, of course, as employing a lawyer familiar with Turkish law.

The first restriction concerns where in Turkey you are allowed to buy a property. As a foreigner, you are only permitted to buy freehold property within the boundaries of a large town or municipal area.

Further restrictions rule out the possibility of buying close to Turkish army bases within a military zone. If an area is declared protected, it is essential that as a foreigner you seek permission from the army headquarters before proceeding with a purchase. It is also necessary to get permission from the local police headquarters. The required funds for buying a property in Turkey, plus any amount needed for purchase taxes, must be transferred from outside Turkey in foreign currency.

The first step to be taken when buying a property is to sign an

FIRST CHOICE FOR YOUR HOME IN TURKEY

Beautiful scenery, attractive coastline, historical interest and plenty of sun have made Turkey the place to go for something different. In association with Pozcu and Collard, Tavnerstar have eleven developments located throughout the Bodrum Peninsular. Rigid planning regulations limit building in town to 2 storeys and outside town to 3 storeys ensuring that the area remains unspoilt. In addition to Bodrum are the luxury developments of Maya village and the Izmir Hilton Golf and Country Club. Prices range from £18,000 to in excess of £100,000 inclusive of tax, registry and notary fees.

For more information visit one of our exhibitions or telephone Dick Schrader now:

01-549 4251

——— TAVNERSTAR LIMITED ———

Dominic House, 171-177 London Road, Kingston-upon-Thames, Surrey KT2 6RA.
Telex: 918417 STARAD G. Fax: 01-546 5222.

---

agreement, or *Gayrimenkul Satis Vaadi Sozlesmesi*, prepared by a notary public. On signing this agreement, the purchaser promises to transfer the agreed amount of money for the property, and the seller promises to transfer the property to the buyer. Although this step is not obligatory, you should insist that the vendor enters this contract with you in order to gain maximum protection under Turkish law, particularly if you are buying a property still under construction and paying instalments in advance. The transaction is completed on signing the final agreement drawn up by the local land registration officer at the local land registration office.

The costs incurred include stamp duty payable at 0.5 per cent of the purchase price, registration fees at around 0.4 per cent and notarial fees at 0.7 per cent. For freehold properties there is also a tax payable on purchase, payable by both vendor and purchaser, of 4 per cent. Legal fees are usually between 1 and 2 per cent. After the initial purchase costs, there is an annual property tax payable at 0.4 per cent of the value of the property. If the property is new, however, a quarter of the annual tax value is exempt from tax for the first five years. These figures are only an indication of the costs incurred and should be checked at the time of purchase.

Selling

If and when you come to selling a property in Turkey, the sum of the funds brought into the country for purchasing the property may be repatriated provided you have the documentary evidence to show that the original funds were brought in through the correct banking channels. Any profit made on resale, however, will be held in the Central Bank of Turkey, and can only be used within the country. It may be some consolation to hear that this sum will not be subject to tax.

CHAPTER 10
MALTA

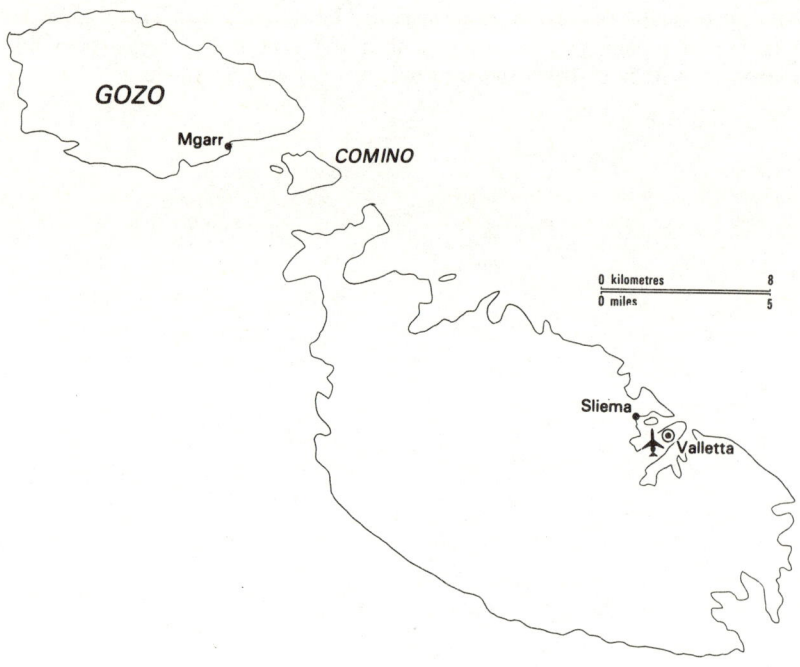

Set in the clear blue waters of the Mediterranean, 60 miles south of Sicily, Malta and its smaller sister island, Gozo, offer a superb year-round climate with long, hot summers and short, mild winters. Temperatures rarely fall below 60°F, even in the coldest months of January and February. The warmth of the sun, coupled with the warmth of the Maltese people, most of whom speak perfect English, have attracted a sizeable community of British residents to the island.

Inevitably, as a small, strategically placed island Malta has had a history of foreign domination, including British rule from 1800 to 1964. The Phoenicians passed through, followed by the Carthaginians, Romans, Arabs, Normans, Spaniards, and then, in a period of more formal colonial power, the Knights of St John, the French and finally the British. All have left their mark on the island, but it was the British naval and strategic interests that largely moulded the island's character, developing the magnificent Grand Harbour area beside the capital, Valletta. It was under British rule, in 1942, that the islanders' bravery in withstanding months of fierce German and Italian bombardment, earned the whole island the honour of the George Cross.

The legacy of 160 years of British colonialism is a familiar, welcoming environment in which to holiday or make a permanent base. Not only is English widely spoken, but many television and radio programmes are in English, as is the daily *Malta Times*. Even telephone and electricity bills are in English; the libraries stock English books; polo, racing and cricket are keenly supported; and the locals drive – most of the time – on the left-hand side of the road. Added to this, the cost of living is among the cheapest in Europe – as is the cost of housing.

In recent years, despite Malta's many attractions, it has been a buyer's market for holiday and retirement homes on the island. Until the election of the pro-British Nationalist party in May 1987, a somewhat unpredictable political climate from the seventies onwards had discouraged foreigners from buying property, and indeed from visiting the island at all. British tourist figures dropped dramatically by over a third in the early 1980s; property that sold was at a fraction of the price of equivalent properties elsewhere in the Mediterranean.

Now confidence has been restored; tourist figures are up, as are the number of foreigners buying property. The new government, led by Prime Minister Eddie Fenech Adami, is determined to forge a new identity for the George Cross island and has launched an aggressive campaign to improve the infrastructure and aim for quality. Included in this campaign is a policy positively to encourage five thousand foreigners to settle permanently on the island over a period of five years. This new permanent residence scheme, together with reciprocal health and taxation agreements between Malta and the United Kingdom, makes the island an attractive choice for those considering early retirement. The price of property, still cheap in comparison with, say, the Costa del Sol or the Algarve, also makes it an attractive choice for a holiday home.

Malta is easily accessible from the UK in just over three hours by air. There are regular scheduled flights from Gatwick and Heathrow and chartered flights from fifteen provincial airports throughout the year. Once on the island, you can travel from one end to the other by bus for just a few pence. Car hire is among the cheapest in Europe.

Valletta and Sliema

Despite the ferocity of the bombardments during the Second World War, many of the island's fine old buildings survived. The capital, Valletta, built by the French Grandmaster of the Order of St John, Jean de la Vallette, dominates in one wide sweep the island's historic Grand Harbour, one of the finest natural harbours in the Mediterranean. Thirty years ago, the grey warships of the Royal Navy would have dominated the scene; today cruise liners, yachts and old *dghajsas* resembling Venetian gondolas line the quaysides, colourful against the soft yellow limestone of the sixteenth-century buildings.

Modern-day Sliema, with its neighbouring St Julian's and St George's areas, lies just north and south of Valletta. It's the largest and most modern town in Malta, a fashionable and sophisticated residential area. Two miles of promenade line the seafront, with pavement cafés, restaurants and shops. It has a casino, hotels and plenty of nightspots.

The Valletta and Sliema conurbation, crowded on to finger-like peninsulas and spreading inland, contains over two hundred thousand people, two-thirds of the total population of the island. Its restaurants, shops and banking facilities make it the most expensive area on the island, although property prices are still very reasonable. A two- or even three-bedroomed apartment can be picked up for as little as £25,000, a terraced three-bedroomed house for around £55,000. Depending on quality, some properties, of course, fetch much higher prices; the majority of the villas on the island cost under £100,000, but at the top end of the market an exceptional villa with private pool and tennis court could fetch as much as £300,000.

Properties on the waterfront enjoy wonderful views of the harbour and passing yachts, and are particularly popular for those considering permanent residence. For yachtsmen, an ambitious project is underway to develop two new marinas with eight hundred and ten thousand berths respectively on the shoreline of Manoel Island, right in the centre of Valletta's natural harbour.

Although there has been some new development following the depressed market in the early 1980s, and more is definitely in the pipeline, the property market in Malta is still largely a resale market. You won't find many 'golf urbanizations' or luxurious purpose-built holiday developments as you might in Spain, but you will get plenty for your money. Good Catholic Maltese tend to have large families and this is reflected in the dimensions of their homes. Studios and one-bedroomed flats are virtually unheard of on the island, and even the most modest two-bedroomed flat, either in a small block or in a complex with gardens and a pool, will have spacious hallways and proper-sized bedrooms with room to walk about in. Generally speaking, you won't find many apartments under 1000 square feet.

Valletta and Sliema

2–3 bed apartment	£25,000–50,000
terraced 3–4 bed house	£55,000–100,000
semi-detached 3–4 bed house	£55,000–150,000
detached 3–4 bed house	£75,000–200,000

Country properties

Malta is shaped rather like a wedge of cheese, with a rind of rugged cliffs and rocky coves in the south-west, sloping down to creeks and sandy bays on the populated north-eastern coast. The island has no mountains and

NEW PERMANENT RESIDENCY SCHEME

The Malta Government has published the new conditions for permanent residency in Malta, amongst which are:
* 15% flat rate of income tax
* death duties only on Malta assets
* many duty free concessions

For full details and a copy of our regular monthly newspaper kindly contact our offices.

SALES AND VALUATIONS OF IMMOVABLE PROPERTY

Our sales department is staffed with a team of sales representatives who have been expertly trained and have gained vast experience in dealing with property matters including: valuations, negotiations and finalisation of sales in Malta and Gozo.

MALTA 2 Paceville Ave., Paceville. Tel: 334418, 337373, 336175, 338775
171 Cospicua Road, Paola. Tel: 782417, 775958.   FAX: 318037

no rivers – just a patchwork of terraced fields, ancient rubble walls, and a sprinkling of evergreen carob and olive trees.

It is half the size of the Isle of Wight, and the longest distance on the island, from north-eastern tip to south-west, is just 16 miles, yet it doesn't take long before an island mentality sets in and alters one's perspective of distance. Anything outside the main hub of activity around the capital is considered out in the sticks, and sells at a discounted price. It is in Malta's sleepy villages, scattered the breadth of the island, that some of the best and most interesting buys can be found. Many British people have made their homes among these clusters of solid, mellow limestone dwellings, and have been welcomed into the community by the locals.

In an attempt to keep at least some houses within the grasp of the islanders themselves, the Maltese government insists that foreigners can only buy property valued at more than Lm8000 (approximately £14,000). The supply of farmhouses or ancient village houses that haven't yet been converted is dwindling year by year, but occasionally a derelict property comes on to the market for less than the permitted figure. This shouldn't pose a problem provided the total amount spent on the property, including the cost of renovation, raises the price above the threshold.

The potential for converting one of these ancient dwellings into a modern, comfortable home, still oozing with old-world character, is enormous. The farmhouses, unlike their British counterparts, are rarely surrounded by fields, but look inwards to a leafy courtyard with old stone benches and a well, and are usually close to the centre of the village. Typically, they have thick, solid walls, vaulted arches, and perhaps an attractive carved stone balcony looking out on to the street. Renovated versions, with modern kitchen and bathroom, can cost anything from £30,000 upwards, depending on the size and quality of conversion.

As well as farmhouses there are so-called 'character houses', meaning converted windmills, knights' hunting lodges and palazzos with private chapels. A property built right in the bastions of Malta's medieval citadel, for instance, was on the market for £140,000. It is common for buyers of such properties to inherit with it the services of a local maid who, like her mother before her, will insist on tending for the property, and do so with loyal affection.

Country properties

3 bed village house, converted	£30,000–60,000
4 bed village house, converted	£50,000–90,000
4 bed 'character' townhouse, converted	£60,000–120,000
6–8 bed historic palazzo, converted	£180,000–300,000

Gozo

Although only 26 square miles in area, Gozo should in no way be dismissed as Malta's little sister island. With a character quite distinctly its own, Gozo is greener, more spectacular and quieter than Malta, saved from the ravages of tourism by virtue of not having an airport.

Gozo presents the restful, unpretentious nature of Mediterranean life. The people are renowned for their hospitality and friendliness. Most live from farming and fishing: the island is famed for its oranges, tomatoes, figs, olives and melons, as well as its tuna, swordfish and lampuki. From the island's flat-topped hills, cultivated valleys stretch out in a patchwork of tiny fields, still tilled by horse and plough. Huge Baroque churches dominate the landscape. The rugged coastline is penetrated by steep valleys and beautiful sandy bays.

Here, as in Malta, farmhouses and ancient dwellings can be found in Gozo's dozen or so villages, strung out on rocky ridges overlooking the valleys and the sea. The opportunity for renovating an ancient property is greater than on Malta, but the prices are a little higher. New development on the island is being tightly controlled, but there are nevertheless, several apartment and villa developments that have sprung up in the last couple of years. On a high ridge near the old Gozitan village of Zebbug, for instance, modern two-bedroomed apartments are selling from

£33,000. At Xlendi, a tiny fishing village on the western coast, two-bed apartments start at £24,000, three-bedroom villas at £48,000.

Gozo

2 bed apartment, newly built	£20,000–45,000
3 bed apartment, newly built	£25,000–50,000
3 bed semi-detached villa, newly built	£50,000–70,000
3 bed detached villa, newly built	£55,000–80,000
3 bed village house, converted	£40,000–80,000
4 bed village house, converted	£60,000–100,000

The Gozo Channel Company runs a regular ferry and hovermarine service across the three-mile channel from Malta to the island's main port at Mgarr. En route the ferry passes Comino, the tiniest of the archipelago, only one square mile in area. With just a single cosy beach hotel and no cars to disturb the peace, Comino enjoys a real 'get-away-from-it-all' atmosphere. Its shallow turquoise waters, clear as crystal, are perfect for snorkelling and diving.

Residence status

Under the Acquisition of Immovable Property regulations introduced by the Maltese government in January 1988, foreigners are allowed to buy only one property in Malta or Gozo. They must opt for one of the following residence statuses: non-residents, temporary residents or permanent residents.

If you buy a property just for holiday use, naturally you will be non-resident status. As such, you may visit Malta for up to three months at a time on the strength of an entry visa which is automatically granted to all British citizens on arrival. Providing you spend less than six months of any year in Malta, you will not be taxed on income you bring to the islands. The only restriction is that the value of the property you buy must exceed Lm8000 (approximately £14,000).

If you wish to live permanently in Malta you may opt for either temporary or permanent residence. As a temporary resident, you are required to show proof that your income will enable you to live in Malta without becoming a burden on the government. Once this requirement is met, you simply apply to the immigration authorities to renew your entry visa once a year. The majority of British people living in Malta do so as temporary residents. Generally, they are subject to local tax conditions only if their stay exceeds six months in one continuous period. Calculated on a sliding scale between 5 and 65 per cent, this is levied only on income actually brought into Malta. As an example, a married couple bringing in Lm4000 (approximately £7000) will be taxed, after deducting Lm1730 married person's allowance, at 13·6 per cent on the remaining balance, equivalent to Lm544 (approximately £940). The double taxation agreement between Malta and the UK prevents tax being paid twice on the same income. Again, the value of the property bought in Malta must exceed Lm8000.

The final and most attractive option for those with incomes over £17,000 or so is to obtain a permanent residence permit. In an attempt to encourage foreigners, particularly wealthy ones, to reside permanently on the island, the Maltese government has halved the maximum income tax rate for permanent residents from 30 per cent to 15 per cent.

To qualify for this tax concession, you must either have an annual income of Lm10,000 (approximately £17,000) anywhere in the world, or a proven capital of Lm150,000 (approximately £225,000). This capital does not have to be brought into Malta except for the amount needed to buy a property. The minimum annual income to be remitted to Malta is Lm6000 for one person, plus Lm1000 for each dependant. A married couple would have to bring in Lm7000 (approximately £12,000). Annual tax liability as a permit holder is 15 per cent of income brought into Malta less personal allowances, or Lm1000, whichever is the higher.

Malta is not, however, a member of the EC. Whether you choose temporary or permanent resident's status, you will not be granted a work permit in Malta unless authorized by the Maltese government.

Buying

Property purchase in Malta and Gozo is a straightforward procedure that shouldn't pose any problems provided you stick to a few government-imposed rules. First, the funds for purchasing a property must originate from outside the country, and, secondly, properties other than those with swimming pools should not be rented out for financial gain. The rules regarding villas with pools were only relaxed recently. Foreigners may let them out provided they apply for a renting licence, costing approximately £590 a year.

A number of properties in Malta require an amount to be paid annually as ground rent. This indicates that the property is leasehold, but does not mean that the lease will run out after a few years, with the title returning to the leaseholder, as it would in the UK. In Malta, properties are sold with a perpetual leasehold that runs for ever, with no change to the amount of ground rent payable each year. If you would prefer, however, you can usually buy the freehold by paying, at the time of purchasing the property, an amount equivalent to twenty times the ground rent.

Having decided on a property, the procedure is to sign a preliminary agreement and pay a deposit of 10 per cent. The agreement is legally binding on both buyer and seller, subject to good title and the issue of the required permits.

The preliminary agreement is usually valid for three months, or longer if agreeable to both parties. During this time a Maltese notary public will undertake the necessary searches, as well as submit all the necessary applications to the relevant government departments. Once all permits have been issued and the title cleared the final deed of the sale is signed, the money handed over and the property yours. All agreements and contracts are in English.

The costs incurred include duty on documents at 3·55 per cent of the purchase price, notary's fees at 1 per cent and a fixed Ministry of Finance fee of around £170. If you buy leasehold, there is also a once-only recognition fee called a Laudemium, equivalent to one year's ground rent payable to the original owner of the land.

Selling

If and when you decide to sell a property, you are obliged to offer it on the local market first before offering it outside the country. For this reason it is always a good idea to buy a property which a local person would consider favourably for his or her own home. There is no capital gains tax in Malta, and no problem repatriating the full proceeds of the sale, including the profit, provided the original funds were brought in through the right channels.

CHAPTER 11
ANDORRA

Nestling high in the Pyrenees, tucked away between France and Spain, the principality of Andorra is hardly the size of the Isle of Wight. Just 18 miles from north to south and 22 miles from east to west, it has a population of twelve thousand native Andorrans and thirty-five thousand foreigners, mainly Spanish, French, a few German, American and Portuguese, and about two thousand Brits.

The principality has much to attract foreign residents. On the same latitude as Rome, it enjoys a sunny and warm climate most of the year, with a marked absence of humidity. Even in the winter months when snow covers its mountain peaks, the chill in the air is compensated for by ceaseless blue skies and sunshine.

Its scenery is some of the most striking in Europe, with high remote valleys, impressive mountains, tumbling rivers, lakes and pastureland. Wild flowers – orchids, daffodils and gentians – carpet the gentle slopes in spring. The summer scene is green and lush, giving way to vibrant reds and gold in the autumn. Come the winter, and a fall of soft, powdery snow once again attracts novice and intermediate skiers to the slopes.

Andorra is not a destination for the advanced skier seeing a new challenge at every turn. It is, however, well geared up for the average one-week-a-year skier, with lifts serving 70 miles of piste at Pas de la Casa/Grau Roig, Soldeu-Tartar, Arinsal, Pal and Arcalis.

Weather, glorious scenery and skiing apart, it is the absence of tax and its status as a free port that has drawn outsiders into Andorra. There are no taxes on income, land or property, no inheritance tax and no capital gains tax. Furthermore, there are no banking and exchange controls. Besides tourism and agriculture, Andorra's income is derived from a remarkably low import levy that has made it an international duty-free shop selling spirits and cigarettes, jewellery, watches, perfume, cameras and calculators. The cost of living here is estimated at about a third below that in the United Kingdom, and the skiing is the cheapest in Europe.

Andorra has what must be the most unique constitution of any country in the world. It is a co-principality under the 'monarchy' of two 'princes' outside its border, President Mitterrand of France and the Spanish Bishop of Seu d'Urgell. Although offered the protection of both, in actuality it is controlled by neither. Andorra has maintained strict neutrality and its Parliament, the Consell General, has always held a policy of non-involvement. The principality has no unemployment, no army and virtually no crime. It has only eighty policemen, sixty of whom are employed to patrol the roads.

If there is one criticism of Andorra, it is its relative inaccessibility. It has no airport of its own, so you have to fly to Barcelona and either drive or take a taxi across the border. Alternatively you can fly to Toulouse, and then either hire a car or take the train to Hospitalet, where you have to catch a bus. Either way, travelling from the airport adds a good three hours to the journey. This may sound insufferable, but in fact it takes no longer than travelling to many of the Alpine ski resorts.

With the 1992 Olympics coming up, there are plans to expand the airport just over the Spanish border at Seu d'Urgell. Until then, many people may continue to drive or take the overnight train through France.

Andorra is not a member of the EC, and British people hoping to work there will have a tough time obtaining a permit. It is, however, relatively easy to reside there providing you apply through the right channels, in Catalan. Catalan is the official language, although French and Spanish, and indeed English, are widely spoken. The only qualifications for residence are that you have a genuine wish to become an active member of the community and that you have an income of not less than £5,000 available at all times in a local bank in Andorra. Then all you need is somewhere to live.

One of the great joys of Andorra is that you never need worry that future property development will crowd it beyond recognition. Ninety-two per cent of its mountainous terrain is protected communal land. Of the remaining 8 per cent that is privately owned, nearly seven-eighths has already been developed. Construction is tightly controlled; strict design regulations enforced by the government restrict building heights and insist on stone wall cladding, rounded Pyrenean roof slates and timber beams, in keeping with the natural materials of the region. Modern buildings are, by necessity, well insulated and double glazed against temperatures that can sometimes drop to 13°F on a winter's night.

Because of the shortage of land, all foreigners are limited as to the amount of property he or she can own at one time. Currently this is one apartment or one house (or a plot of building land not exceeding 1000 square metres – about a quarter of an acre). A husband and wife count as a joint entity for this purpose. All property is freehold, and for the last decade or so has enjoyed a steady capital growth of between 10 and 20 per cent a year.

Country properties

Old country barns, or *bordas* as they are called, with stables for the animals downstairs and living quarters above, convert into attractive modern homes and often command the best positions. They are, however, difficult to come by, mainly because there were very few built in the first place. Until after the Second World War, Andorra was an impoverished country supporting a tiny rural population. Old properties that exist are, in most cases, jealously guarded by Andorran families.

Having said that, one or two occasionally come on the market. If you are lucky you might pick up an ancient village house with iron mangers and a dirt floor downstairs, some old rickety steps, and a large upstairs room with a bread oven and an attic above that, for £70,000 or £80,000. Invest another £50,000 or £60,000 and you will have a delightful two-bedroomed house, oozing with character. Renovated *bordas* rarely come up for less than £130,000.

Country Property

3 bed converted *borda*	£130,000–150,000
4–5 bed converted *borda*	£150,000–220,000

New properties

Many of the new developments are geared specifically for holiday use and for investment. Capital growth has been consistent over the years, and rental returns can almost be guaranteed from mid-December to 25 April when traditionally the ski lifts are closed at the end of the season.

Facilities are improving all the time. New ski lifts are opening up new pistes and linking existing resorts, while for the summer a golf course, the first in Andorra, is planned near Lake Engolaster above the village of Encamp.

The skiing is particularly good for families with young children. Most of the instructors speak English (many are, in fact, Australian), and generally Andorra's southerly position ensures warm and sunny conditions for little ones left practising on the nursery slopes. For those with a car, an undoubted attraction is having a choice of five ski resorts all within thirty minutes' drive of the capital, Andorra la Vella.

The most popular choice of property in or near any of the ski stations is apartments. In a climate where night temperatures are very low, apartments offer the obvious advantage of being easy to lock up and leave. Usually they are fitted with automatic heating switches that come on in the event of a freeze, and you can rest assured that a caretaker will always be around to keep an eye on things.

Chalets are also popular, as are purpose-built complexes known as *pletas*. These are rustic estates built in the style of the old *bordas*, with cobbled streets and alleyways. Some have shops and restaurants. The houses often feature open fireplaces and sturdy exposed beams.

Another option is a suite in an aparthotel. Typically, an aparthotel will have a reception area, restaurant, lounge and bar on the ground floor, just like an ordinary hotel, and perhaps some shops and sporting facilities. Upstairs it has fully furnished hotel suites, completely self-contained with kitchenette and bathroom. These can be studios, one- or two-bedroomed. Owners of the suites can either use them as they might a self-contained apartment, or enjoy the restaurant and service facilities of the hotel.

The concept is relatively new in Andorra and has proved an enormous success. Often aparthotels are situated on or near the 'international route' – the main road crossing Andorra from France and Spain. As well as offering the obvious advantage of trouble-free ownership, they generate a good rental income in the summer months as well as in the winter, mainly from French and Spanish tourists enjoying a few days' stopover in Andorra en route from one country to the other.

Anyos Park, a development nestling in a sunny valley about ten minutes' drive from the capital, has taken the concept of the aparthotel one stage further. Here, in addition to the usual facilities on offer, owners have use of a magnificent sports centre with an impressive range of facilities. It has seven squash courts, tennis courts, a pool, shooting, archery, sauna, solarium and gymnasium – just for starters. Needless to say, these facilities go towards ensuring greater rental returns.

For permanent living, many expatriates opt to live in or around La Massana, a town in a wide and open valley just up the road from the capital. La Massana itself offers all the shops, banks and restaurants you might need, in a rural setting just five minutes from the ski slopes at Arinsal. Alternatively, villages in the southern tip of the principality, such as Juberri, Auvinya and Aixirivall, are popular. They face south at a lower altitude, overlooking the valleys of Spain, and again have good access to the capital. Andorra la Vella itself is a busy, commercial town right on the international route.

The prices paid for properties vary enormously with the facilities offered. Aparthotels and *pletas*, for example, tend to be more expensive than no-fuss apartments. Prices also vary depending on whether the property is intended for residential or holiday use. Apartments and chalets built for permanent living tend to be more spacious, they may have more ground, and they tend to be in better locations. Aspect also makes a difference: you can expect to pay more for a south-facing apartment with uninterrupted mountain views.

As an example of the difference in price you can pay, a one-bedroomed apartment can be £35,000 (you won't find much for less) or as much as £110,000. A three-bedroomed apartment could be as low as £70,000 or as high as £235,000, depending largely on whether it is geared at the holiday or residential market. A chalet will cost between £150,000 and £260,000. The following guide gives an idea of average prices in Andorra.

Holiday property

studio	£25,000–37,000
1 bed apartment	£35,000–50,000
2 bed apartment	£47,000–75,000
3 bed apartment	£70,000–90,000

Residential accommodation

2 bed apartment	£65,000–95,000
3 bed apartment	£85,000–150,000
3–4 bed chalet	£150,000–260,000

Buying

As well as no tax on income, capital gains and death, Andorra has virtually no taxes on the transfer of property. The total cost, including notary's and legal fees, is normally between 1.5 and 2 per cent of the purchase price – much cheaper than in either France or Spain.

The usual procedure is to draw up a purchase agreement, signed by both buyer and seller, and pay a non-returnable deposit of 10 per cent of the purchase price. The document can be drawn up in any language to suit the parties concerned. Approximately six weeks later the purchase contract, drawn up in Catalan, is signed by both parties, or their respective powers of attorney, in the presence of an Andorran notary public. The transaction is then fully legal, with all rights passing to the buyer.

There is no obligatory registration of property ownership in Andorra. Nevertheless it is advisable, following completion, to lodge an official ownership document (*escritura*) in the public registration office. If a public title deed is registered in this way, it is necessary to have authorization from the Andorran government.

Selling

This operation is just as simple and inexpensive as buying in the first place. There are no problems repatriating the money, and no capital gains tax.

CHAPTER 12
IRELAND

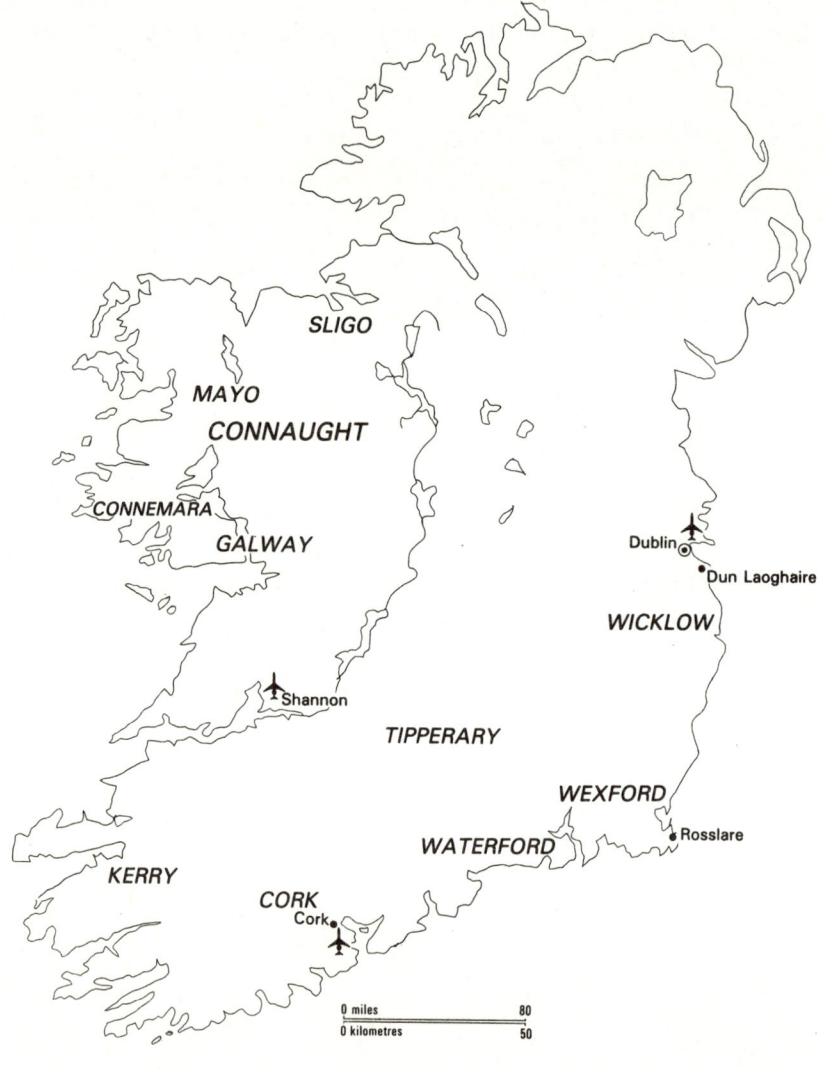

It is no surprise that Eire – to use Ireland's ancient, Celtic name – is called the Emerald Isle. Its stunning shamrock green is the product of a mild, humid and ever-changing climate created by the Atlantic weather washing over one of Europe's most westerly islands. Warm fronts sweep in from the ocean at any time of the year, drenching the countryside beneath sheets of low cloud. In the mountainous west, the rainfall varies from 40 inches a year on the coast to twice that or more in the mountains. 'The sun may not shine, but the rain is warm,' they say. Then a cold front will arrive, bringing bright skies that endow the landscape with a sparkling brilliance of colour.

But despite the unpredictability of the weather, millions of tourists visit Ireland each year. Many are of Irish descent, returning to their roots. Others go just for the wonderful, unspoilt beauty of the land and the lakes, the friendly, hospitable people, and the relaxed atmosphere and change of pace. It's a haven for walking, fishing, shooting, golf – Ireland has approaching two hundred golf courses, many set in the most spectacular coastal scenery – or for simply getting away from it all.

Apart from the sporting life, Ireland also seems determined to encourage and nurture its cultural heritage. It has, of course, contributed immeasurably in the past: Sheridan, Yeats, Shaw, Oscar Wilde and James Joyce are just a few of Ireland's literary giants that have enthralled readers and theatregoers for generations. Today, a rather quaint tax-free regime exists for artists, writers and musicians who reside in Ireland and can persuade the Revenue Commissioners' independent panel of experts that their work is of 'cultural or artistic merit'. Introduced in 1969, this tax-free regime also includes the fees from stallions at stud, making Ireland the centre of the multi-billion-pound European bloodstock industry.

A number of poets, actors, writers, even pop stars have bought property in Ireland, drawn by the freedom from tax. However, the majority of non-Irish buyers are people attracted by the sheer good value of the property. Although the cost of living is estimated at about 10 per cent above that in the UK, the price of property, outside Dublin, is roughly half or even a third that of equivalent properties in England. A small but sturdy cottage on the west coast can still be picked up for around IR£25,000, a four-bedroomed Georgian country house for as little as IR£70,000–80,000. These prices become even more attractive when you consider that the Irish 'punt' is worth only about 85 pence.

Having said property is cheap, there has recently been something of a property boom in Ireland, following a static period of seven or eight years. A greater confidence in the economy and low inflation, coupled with availability of finance and low interest rates relative to the UK, released a long pent-up demand for certain types of property, particularly up-market property in Dublin and in the large country house market. Price gains, however, have not been evenly spread. There have been isolated instances of Dublin houses increasing in value by up to 50 per cent in two years, while country cottages, ideal for holiday homes, have generally shown more modest increases of around 5–10 per cent.

As well as a property boom, the last couple of years have seen a major air travel boom in Ireland. Competition on air fares and services has radically altered the cost and frequency of flights to and from Ireland. There has been an increase in the number of regular flights to Dublin,

Cork and Shannon, and a halving of the price. A return ticket can now cost as little as £60 or £70. In addition, regional airports at Knock (Connaught), Galway and Waterford have been upgraded and now run direct flights to London and regional airports in the United Kingdom. For those wishing to take their car across the water, there are regular car ferry services from Swansea to Cork, from Pembroke and Fishguard to Rosslare Harbour, and from Holyhead to Dublin and Dun Laoghaire.

Country properties

Of the 140,000 or so UK citizens living in the Republic of Ireland, about half live in the capital, Dublin; but they are there mainly for business. For holiday homes, most head for the varied and beautiful Irish countryside, more especially around the coastal regions.

To the north and west is the wild and beautiful province of Connaught, including the counties of Sligo, Mayo and Galway and the blue lakes and changing-coloured mountains of Connemara. Totally unspoilt, with long coral beaches, lakes, islands and twisting country lanes, this whole area offers some of the most dramatic coastal scenery anywhere in the world. A friend who's a fly-fishing champion tells me the game fishing in Connaught matches anywhere in the British Isles; the limestone loughs of Mask, Conn and Corrib are particularly well favoured. Some of Ireland's best-known golf courses are also within the region. At one time a journey to these parts involved taking a flight to Dublin or Shannon followed by a long drive across country. Today you can fly direct to Galway or to Knock – the latter is situated in one of the bleakest bogs you will ever have seen, but is nevertheless convenient!

Along this stretch of coastline and further south in County Kerry and Cork, where long Atlantic-probing peninsulas are backed by the towering peaks of the Caha and Slieve Mish mountains, derelict country cottages, ripe for conversion, are going for a song. An ancient stone-built croft, stripped of its original thatched roof, with perhaps an acre of land overlooking the sea, can be picked up for between £5000 and £10,000. A similar building, unmodernized but just about habitable with two bedrooms and a slate roof to keep out the rain, costs between £15,000 and £20,000. The Irish hate them, regarding them as impractical and expensive to keep up, but, converted, they make idyllic, romantic retreats for mad Englishmen. A comfortable, modernized two-bedroomed cottage costs around £25,000–30,000.

As well as small country cottages, Ireland has a wealth of Victorian and Georgian country houses scattered the breadth of the island from the western hills to the mild east coast south of Dublin. It is the Irish country house, together with up-market Dublin property, that has shot up in price in the last year or so. However, in the rolling countryside of County Wicklow, close to Dublin, it is still possible to pick up a minor Georgian mansion – the sort that would command upwards of quarter of a million pounds in London's ever-growing commuter belt – for no more than £160,000 or £170,000.

Further from Dublin, the price of properties in rural areas can be assumed to be much the same throughout the country. In County Wexford, for instance, a comfortable eight-bedroomed Georgian country house with two and a half acres of land was recently on the market for £80,000. In Tipperary, a delightful four-bedroomed Georgian house with an acre of grounds, garaging and stables cost just £85,000; and, with approaching 200 acres of land included in the price, a four-bedroomed farmhouse with tree-lined avenue and lawned gardens, just seven miles from Waterford airport, cost £260,000.

Country properties

2 bed cottage, in state of ruin	£5,000–10,000
2 bed cottage, unmodernized	£15,000–20,000
2 bed cottage, renovated	£25,000–30,000
4 bed country house	£60,000–70,000
5–6 bed country house + 5 acres	£70,000–100,000
7–8 bed country house + 25 acres	£100,000–220,000

Buying

With the exception of a few minor differences in terminology, buying a property in Ireland is little different from buying a property in England. You will find, for example, that estate agents are more commonly referred to as auctioneers, and that contracts are 'signed' rather than 'exchanged', and 'closed' rather than 'completed'. Otherwise, the only significant difference is the stamp duty payable on purchase. This is higher than in England, with rates ranging from 2 per cent of purchase price to a maximum of 6 per cent on properties valued at over £60,000. New properties are exempt. Also, non-Irish buyers must apply for permission from the Irish Land Commission. This, however, is only a formality unless the property has over five acres and is intended for more than residential purposes.

Selling

There are no problems regarding repatriation of funds emanating from the sale of a property in Ireland. If, however, the property is sold for more than it was bought for and is not your principal residence, you will be subject to capital gains tax. This varies from 30 per cent for properties held over six years to a maximum of 60 per cent for properties sold within a year. Tax liability can be reduced by setting against profit an annual exemption (not restricted to residents) of IR£2000 (single person) or IR£4000 (married person), and any transaction costs. The sale price, and thus chargeable gain, will also be adjusted to allow for inflation.

CHAPTER 13
SKI RESORTS

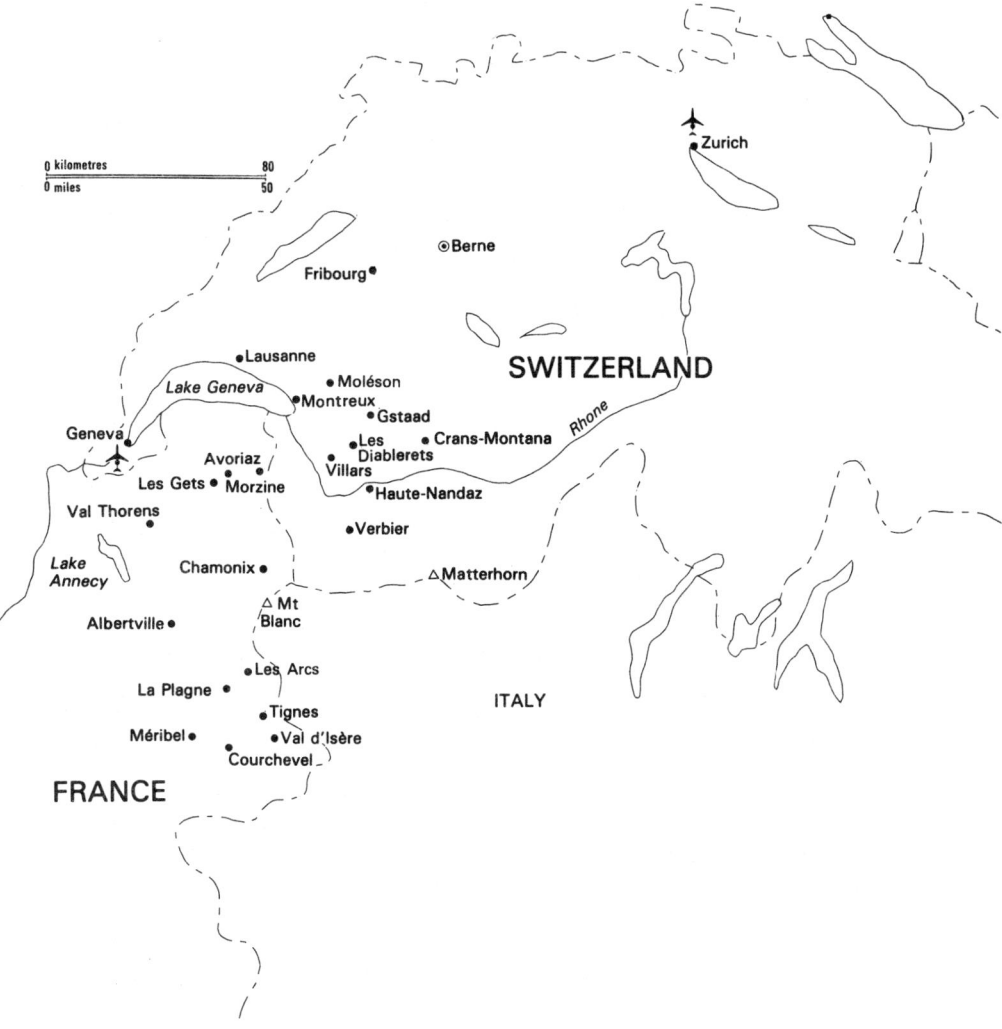

Skiing isn't just a sport, it's an addiction. Once hooked, skiers find themselves forking out hundreds, sometimes thousands of pounds for their annual fix on the slopes, much to the joy of winter tour operators. In the last few years, the British have taken to the pistes with a growing enthusiasm almost matching that of their fellow Europeans. Along with the growing ski holiday market, the market for ski apartments and chalets has exploded in the same way that the sun and sea property market did ten years ago.

For the committed skier, the advantages of buying a home in the mountains are obvious. You can ski whenever you like, for as long as you like, without having to worry about the extra expense of high season months. In addition, you can expect a good rental income from other skiers, provided the apartment or chalet is well located for the ski lifts and other resort facilities. Furthermore, you need never again lug your skis and boots back and forth on the plane or on the roof of your car.

The range of ski apartments and chalets available, particularly in the different resorts in France, Switzerland and Austria, is enormous. Restrictions imposed on foreign property buyers in the Swiss and Austrian Alps, however, mean that by far the largest market is in France. No other region has rushed to satisfy the demand for ski apartments quite like the Savoie and Haute-Savoie regions of the northern French Alps.

France

Savoie

Mostly above tree level, the high-altitude slopes of the Savoie region offer some of the most extensive and challenging ski runs anywhere in the world. Names of resorts in the region such as Val d'Isère, Courchevel, Tignes and Val Thorens trip off the tongue of anyone who has so much as glanced through a winter holiday brochure. They are among the established meccas of the ski world.

Of the 2 million or so beds in ski resorts throughout France, the majority are in the Savoie region. Resorts have sprung up solely for the purpose of skiing, and hundreds of millions of francs have been invested in cable cars, chair lifts and pommels reaching to the highest peaks of the mountains. Anyone who has skied the area cannot help but be impressed by the facilities both on and off the piste, yet in the next couple of years a further 7 billion francs will be invested in the area. It is in the Savoie region, centred on Albertville, that in 1992 the Winter Olympic Games will be held.

There is hardly a resort that will not benefit in some way or another from this great event. In Albertville itself two Olympic skating rinks are being built; in Courchevel, a ski jump; and in La Plagne, an artificial bobsleigh run. Tignes will host the ski ballet; Méribel and Val d'Isère the downhill events; Les Ménuires and Val Thorens the slalom events; and Les Arcs, the *ski de vitesse* or 'flying 100 metres', where madmen risk their necks at speeds of 130mph.

The frenzy of activity building up to the Games is enormous, involving not just the construction and upgrading of sporting facilities but also the building of still more apartments and improving accessibility to the resorts. Permanent benefits should result, since major road improvements are being made and a second international terminal is being added to Lyon airport. Although Lyon is used mainly for scheduled rather than chartered flights, with luck the second terminal might relieve some of the horrendous traffic through Geneva airport on the weekly changeover days in the winter months. At present, most of the resorts are a three- or four-hour drive from Geneva airport

Val d'Isère
Perhaps the best-known resort in the Savoie Alps is Val d'Isère. Known affectionately as 'Val', it's a popular resort with the English, offering excellent restaurants, bars and sporting facilities in new and old-style buildings centred around the eleventh-century Savoyard church. Linked with neighbouring Tignes to form the famous L'Espace Killy, Val d'Isère offers an incredible 250 miles of pistes. The season is long, with skiing from November to early May and glacier skiing in July and August.

As in most resorts in France, the accommodation in Val d'Isère is mainly in the form of apartments. Prices have shot up recently, doubling in the space of five years and making it one of the most expensive French resorts in which to buy property. Studios are now virtually unheard of in Val d'Isère, and one-bedroomed apartments are few and far between. Most new properties coming on to the market are two- or three-bedroomed, well appointed and with good-sized rooms. Prices vary enormously, depending on accessibility to the ski lifts and the centre of town.

Val d'Isère

1 bed apartment	£70,000–100,000
2 bed apartment	£90,000–130,000
3 bed apartment	£120,000–250,000

Tignes
It's no good looking for an old village centre in Tignes. It was drowned long ago with the creation of a huge dam which flooded the valley, forming the Lac du Chevril. The reborn Tignes lies in a wide basin above the Isère valley, surrounded by impressive, rather austere mountains dominated by the Grande Motte. It is very much a purpose-built resort with modern apartment blocks, offering the superb year-round skiing of L'Espace Killy. It's here that the British World Cup Team undertakes its rigorous training. Ski runs radiate from the village, making it possible to plan a day's skiing to follow the sun. It has a young and lively atmosphere with good restaurants and bars.

Although new properties are becoming scarcer by the year in Tignes, studio, one-, two- and occasionally three-bedroomed apartments are available at more reasonable prices than in Val d'Isère. Note that when the French refer to *deux pièces* they mean one-bedroomed, *trois pièces* means two-bedroomed, and so on. A *deux pièces* apartment is often marketed as sleeping four people: two in the bedroom and two on sofa beds in the living room!

Tignes

studio apartment	£35,000–50,000
1 bed apartment	£40,000–65,000
2 bed apartment	£65,000–85,000
3 bed apartment	£100,000–130,000

Val Thorens
At 7500 feet Val Thorens is the highest resort in Europe, with an excellent snow record and long hours of sunshine. It is also the newest resort in Les Trois Vallées, a vast snowfield with some two hundred lifts and over 300 miles of prepared pistes. Compact and entirely purpose-built, it's a traffic-free resort with skiing to and from the door. The skiing is rated among the best in the world.

Although quieter than many resorts, Val Thorens has several good restaurants and bars and a sports complex with indoor tennis and squash courts. It has twelve hundred beds and plans to expand to no more than eighteen hundred. This is one of the reasons it is renowned for its lack of queues. It is first and foremost a skier's resort.

Val Thorens

studio apartment	£35,000–50,000
1 bed apartment	£40,000–65,000
2 bed apartment	£65,000–85,000
3 bed apartment	£100,000–130,000

Courchevel
Set among pine trees in a natural amphitheatre, Courchevel is the most beautiful and the most sophisticated of resorts. Again in Les Trois Vallées, it has superb skiing – both downhill and cross-country – which usually continues well into April. It also has the best aprés-ski in the Alps: numerous restaurants, nightclubs, piano bars, pubs and cafés. Here you can play 'spot the famous face', and go shopping (or window shopping) in fashionable boutiques.

Courchevel consists of three purpose-built resorts: Courchevel 1850, 1650 and 1550, plus the original village of Courchevel. The highest and most fashionable of these, Courchevel 1850 is one of the most expensive places you could choose to buy an apartment in France. Prices here have doubled in five years. In Courchevel 1650 and 1550, however, prices are considerably cheaper. An hourly shuttle bus links the resorts, or you can toboggan, slide or ski – but only to the lower resorts! If driving to the slopes from the airport seems too much of a bore, you can take an air taxi or helicopter direct to Courchevel's own altiport.

Courchevel 1850

1 bed apartment	£150,000–180,000
2 bed apartment	£200,000–250,000
3 bed apartment	£300,000–400,000

Courchevel 1650 and 1550

1 bed apartment	£60,000–80,000
2 bed apartment	£110,000–140,000
3 bed apartment	£130,000–170,000

Haute-Savoie

Portes du Soleil
Beautifully situated between Mont Blanc and Lake Geneva, the Portes du Soleil straddles the border between France and Switzerland, offering some 400 miles of pistes in fourteen valleys.

Although not as high as the Savoie Alps, the skiing is nevertheless good and the scenery quite spectacular. Much of it lies below tree level; it's gentler, more human in scale. Portes du Soleil is a summer as well as a winter resort. Close to Lake Geneva and Lake Annecy, it offers a wide range of watersport activities as well as tennis and golf. Then there are the mountains themselves, providing opportunities to take in the breathtaking views on gentle walks or to do serious mountaineering; Mont Blanc itself is a dominating feature at 15,782 feet.

The only purpose-built skiing resort in Portes du Soleil is Avoriaz, set high in the mountains at 7000 feet. Otherwise all the resorts are centred around old-established Alpine villages. Morzine, for instance, is a picturesque huddle of wooden-clad chalets with a lively though unsophisticated atmosphere. It offers excellent ski facilities with an interlinking lift system providing access to other resorts in the Portes du Soleil, including Avoriaz. Les Gets is the next village of any size to Morzine and is one of the oldest resorts in the Portes du Soleil circuit. Again it has enormous charm and several excellent restaurants, and offers good downhill skiing as well as 16 miles of cross-country trails. All the resorts are within a short drive of Geneva airport.

Typically, apartments in Portes du Soleil are in timber-clad chalets, often with balconies, designed in sympathy with the older properties in the Alpine villages where they are located. Apartments from studio size

to *trois pièces et mézzanine* are available, as well as individual chalets. Prices vary, depending on accessibility to the slopes and amenities in the villages, but are generally cheaper than properties of equivalent site in the Savoie region.

Portes du Soleil

studio apartment	£25,000–35,000
1 bed apartment	£35,000–55,000
2 bed apartment	£45,000–80,000
2 bed chalet	£55,000–90,000
3–4 bed chalet	£80,000–150,000

Chamonix valley

One of the Alps' magical names, Chamonix is smart and traditional with wonderful shops and restaurants. It sits at the foot of Mont Blanc, just a tunnel away from Italy and only forty minutes from Geneva. An old town full of character and charm, Chamonix is both a summer and winter resort. There is superb skiing, both downhill and cross-country, in the

Chamonix valley, while for the summer months there is an 18-hole golf course, tennis, swimming, riding, rock-climbing, mountaineering and hang-gliding.

For a smart resort, property can be bought at remarkably unsmart prices. In an attractive rambling Savoyard apartment chalet, for instance, in a central position by the river, a one-bedroomed apartment costs around £35,000, a two-bedroomed apartment £63,000. If you are prepared to stand while you eat and sleep, an elegant broom cupboard of a studio measuring just 15 feet by 9 feet can be picked up for as little as £16,000.

Chamonix valley

studio apartment	£25,000–40,000
1 bed apartment	£30,000–50,000
2 bed apartment	£55,000–80,000

Leaseback

If the likelihood is that you could only make full use of a ski apartment for six or eight weeks of the year, an attractive option might be to buy a freehold apartment under a leaseback arrangement. In essence, this scheme offers significant reductions in the purchase price in return for surrendering rental rights to the developer, or a rental agency acting for the developer, for a period of nine or eleven years. During the leaseback period you have use of the apartment for a fixed number of weeks a year. At the end of the leaseback period, full possession and use of the apartment reverts to you, or you may, by mutual agreement, embark upon a further leaseback period. The scheme has proved an enormous success in France, with some 65 per cent of all leisure homes being sold in this way.

Various permutations of the leaseback method of purchase exist, but in essence they fall into two categories. The first method, often referred to as *propriété allégée*, is geared at buyers wanting a maximum reduction in price at the time of purchase, while the second method, *placement financier*, offers a smaller reduction in price at the time of purchase, but then guarantees a rental income during the leaseback period.

Under the *propriété allégée* arrangement, for example, you could buy a fully furnished apartment with a 30 per cent reduction on the price. This 30 per cent includes the VAT that is payable on all new properties in France. During the leaseback period you would be allocated use of the apartment for six weeks of the year – two weeks in high season (usually during the French school holidays!), two weeks in mid-season and two weeks in low season. Under the *placement allégée* arrangement you would be offered a lower reduction, often equivalent to the value of the VAT element of the price, which is currently running at 18.6 per cent.

You would then be guaranteed an annual rental on a sliding scale – say between 4 and 5.5 per cent – dependent on the number of weeks you chose to use the apartment yourself. This would usually be between two and eight weeks a year. In both cases, the rental agency is responsible for maintaining and managing the property.

The scheme is well suited to the holiday apartment market. A minor criticism is that the rooms are sometimes small, but there again they are not intended for permanent living.

Switzerland

It's said that the safest and most efficient ski lifts are in Switzerland, followed by France, then Austria, and last of all Italy. Typically, Switzerland sits at the top of the pyramid, small but regular as clockwork in every respect.

For those with a tendency to belt and braces, Switzerland offers as stable an economy and political climate as you will find anywhere in the world. It is spotlessly, almost clinically clean and has a record of virtually no vandalism and no crime. Security isn't a problem, and it's the only place in the world that you stand some chance of survival in a nuclear war. The government states by law that every newly built property has to incorporate a fall-out shelter.

Switzerland is also, of course, a very beautiful country, well worthy of protection. No one can fail to be impressed by its mountains and lakes, its sturdy wooden chalets, its Alpine flowers and brown and white cows with bells round their necks. Perhaps because the Swiss have it so good, they like to keep it to themselves.

The policy of the Swiss Federal Government is to restrict the number of properties available for sale to foreigners. In 1986 permission was granted for just two thousand properties in the whole country to be sold to non-Swiss nationals. In 1987 the number was reduced to eighteen hundred, and in 1988 to around sixteen hundred. The policy is to reduce the quota by around 10 per cent each year, so that, theoretically, the figure could eventually disappear altogether. That is not to say that if the full quota is not sold in one year the remainder cannot be carried over to the next. It can, and often is. The number of permits allocated varies from canton to canton (there are twenty-six cantons, or administrative states, in Switzerland) and from resort to resort. Some cantons issue a steady but diminishing supply, while others refuse to issue permits at all.

The quota system is not the only difficulty facing foreign buyers. There are a mass of other restrictions as well. For instance, a foreigner is allowed to buy only one property. Furthermore, the limit for living accommodation is 100 square metres and the plot size 1000 square metres. (Note, though, that on the point of living accommodation 100 square metres can often be expanded to 140 or 150 square metres by adding on 'non-living' areas such as built-in cupboards, storage space, low head-room in attics, corridors, laundry rooms, ski lockers and so on.)

Also, foreign owners of property are expected to occupy the property for a minimum of three weeks a year, thus ruling out long-term rental contracts of one year or more.

Finally, property bought by a foreigner may not be sold for a specified number of years. Again, this restriction varies from canton to canton. In the majority of cases you are held in for a minimum of five years; in some extreme cases it is ten years, while in others it is two years or none at all. The only circumstances allowing you to sell the property before the specified date are chronic illness or bankruptcy. After the fixed period, you may sell the property to a Swiss national or Swiss resident. At the discretion of the canton you may apply for permission to sell to another foreigner only if you cannot find a Swiss buyer within a given period.

These measures are considered a necessary precaution to discourage property speculation, and in some cases may be so restricting as to make you wonder whether to bother at all. However, investors have always been attracted to Switzerland and will continue to be so for very positive reasons. Switzerland has one of the strongest currencies in the world, added to which Swiss property has historically appreciated by 5–7 per cent a year. Furthermore, for those who get in early, quotas, far from being restricting, may add a scarcity value to their property. Also, money is cheap in Switzerland; it is possible to borrow up to 70 per cent of the purchase price of the property over ten to twenty years, using the Swiss property as security, at interest rates of 6–6.5 per cent.

Property buyers in Switzerland also know they will get good quality for their money. Swiss chalets, with their rows of decorative wooden balconies, are always well built, offering exceedingly high standards of materials and workmanship. Apartments, too, offer the best in insulation and interior fixtures and fittings.

Canton Valais
Renowned as one of the premier ski areas in the Alps, Canton Valais covers a substantial part of southern Switzerland and includes such celebrated resorts as Verbier, Saas Fee, Crans-Montana and Zermatt. It would be top of the list for any ski enthusiast thinking of buying a property in Switzerland, except that in December 1987 there was a local referendum in Valais, the result of which was a ban on all new allocations for property sales to foreigners from the beginning of 1988. That's not to say that permits will not be allocated at some future date, but in the meantime only property allocations left over from past years are available to foreign buyers.

At the last count there were some apartments allocated for foreigners remaining in Crans-Montana, an elegant resort sitting high on a south-facing plateau overlooking the Rhône valley. Here the sun shines on the international jet set both on the piste and off, in the smart hotels, restaurants and nightclubs. It has both winter and summer skiing, as well as two golf courses, tennis, swimming pools and riding, making it a lively, active resort for the full twelve months of the year.

Most of the apartments are in traditional chalet style with timber cladding and balconies. For instance, apartment chalets facing the golf course, tucked away in the pines yet only five minutes' walk from the centre of Crans-Montana, cost for one-bedders £116,000, and for two-bedders £201,000; or, in a small apartment chalet just outside the busy centre, one-bedders £98,000, two-bedders, £136,000.

Crans-Montana

1 bed apartment	£100,000–130,000
2 bed apartment	£130,000–200,000
3 bed apartment	£180,000–280,000

There are also a few allocations remaining at Haute-Nandaz, a lively resort with excellent skiing linked into Les Quatre Vallées. Once a tiny mountain village, Haute-Nandaz has grown beyond recognition but manages to retain much of its original charm since new apartment chalets, large and small, are built in traditional style. It has all the amenities: tennis courts, ice rink, swimming pool, restaurants, bars and a pub.

Canton Vaud

An increasingly popular area for house buyers in Switzerland, Canton Vaud offers excellent skiing at resorts such as Villars, Les Diablerets and Château d'Oex, while enjoying easy access to the fashionable towns of Gstaad, Montreux and Lausanne and to Lake Geneva. It's ideal for both winter and summer holidays and, unlike Canton Valais, continues to issue new allocations for property sales to foreigners.

At Villars, a mountain resort just an hour and a half's drive from Geneva, the skiing has developed enormously in the last few years. Linking with Les Diablerets across the Meilleret ski zone, it provides a total of 75 miles of marked piste, with skiing possible in the summer months as well on the Glacier des Diablerets.

Villars lies in a wide south-facing valley and has plenty of room for building development. Handsome chalets are blossoming everywhere, but tight building regulations ensure that there is no sense of stark over-development; all new buildings have to be of traditional style and clad with wood. Many people, tired of queue-infested, over-developed resorts, are moving to Villars because of its charm and its excellent skiing. It also has an 18-hole golf course and tennis courts, making it an ideal choice for summer holidays as well.

A number of one-, two- and three-bedroomed apartments and newly built chalets are available in Villars for foreign buyers. Generally those in

Switzerland

If you are looking for a sound investment in property, we specialise in high quality developments in well-known locations and more unusual ones

For more advice and information
Contact:
Catherine Law
Projectel
P.O. Box 175
Guildford
GU1 2PL
Tel: (0483) 68846/571226 (24h)

the centre of the town, close to the restaurants, bars and the ski lifts, are more expensive, while property is about 20 per cent cheaper in the satellite villages of Chesières and Barboleuse. The chalets in Chesières and Barboleuse tend to be smaller, typically comprising six or eight apartments; many are positioned right on the piste – superbly located for skiing. The only disadvantage of buying a property in either of these villages is that it would be essential to have a car, whereas in Villars itself you can rely quite happily on the superb Swiss railway service from Geneva.

It is now very rare for an individual chalet to be authorized for sale to foreign buyers, but it is possible to have your own chalet built to specification. A typical chalet, built on three floors with three or four bedrooms, right on the piste, would cost around £330,000–360,000.

Villars

studio apartment	£70,000–110,000
1 bed apartment	£105,000–130,000
2 bed apartment	£125,000–175,000
3 bed apartment	£170,000–250,000
4 bed chalet	£250,000–360,000

Linked by a series of drags and a chairlift to Villars, Les Diablerets is a small, picturesque village facing the majestic glacier of the same name. It is full of Swiss mountain character and charm, with excellent restaurants and fun après-ski, skating, curling, swimming pools – indoor and open air – tennis courts, and, of course, miles and miles of piste, extensive as that of Villars. A small local railway up from Aigle means that a car is not essential.

Several properties in Les Diablerets might be available for sale to foreigners at any one time. For instance, one-bed apartments in a chalet on high ground above the village, price £83,000, and two-bedroomed apartments in the same chalet, £92,000; or in a traditional apartment chalet a stone's throw from the village centre, two-bedroomed apartments £127,000, four-bedroomed duplexes £212,000.

Canton Fribourg
To the north and east of Lake Geneva in the foothills of the Alps, Canton Fribourg is gentle, low-lying and wooded in parts, somewhat reminiscent of the English Lake District. In a book on ski resorts it might barely be worth a mention, but its relatively cheap property, its ample supply of chalets and its relaxed laws concerning foreigners make it irresistible. In Canton Fribourg there are no restrictions governing when and to whom you can sell a property.

To say that there is no skiing in Fribourg would be unfair. There are a few downhill runs, and in the Greyère region mile after mile of cross-country paths, but the only mountain of any significance is Moléson, at about 6600 feet. Otherwise, the nearest slopes are approximately forty minutes' drive away at Château d'Oex.

Canton Fribourg appeals to people looking not so much for a chic resort as for a permanent home. On this subject, permanent residence in Switzerland will only be granted if you are over sixty, your children are over eighteen, and you have adequate proven income. A non-resident can spend a maximum of six months in Switzerland at any one time.

In Moléson village itself, at the foot of the best ski runs in Fribourg, property is reasonably priced by Swiss standards. In a chalet close to the ski lift in the village, for example, a good-sized, two-bedroomed apartment might cost around £80,000, a three-bedroomed apartment around £90,000. A resale chalet with three bedrooms could be picked up for £125,000. Moléson is an hour from Geneva and within easy reach of Vevey, Neuchâtel, Berne and Fribourg town.

Examples of other chalets in the region include a three-bedroomed, fully furnished chalet with lovely views close to Lake Montsalvens, price £140,000. In Charmey, a two-bedroomed chalet close to the village centre costs from £112,000, a three-bedroomed chalet from £130,000.

Canton Fribourg

studio apartment	£30,000–50,000
1 bed apartment	£50,000–70,000
2 bed apartment	£60,000–90,000
3 bed apartment	£80,000–130,000
2 bed chalet	£85,000–130,000
3 bed chalet	£115,000–180,000

Aparthotels

There are some highly desirable resorts such as Klosters and Davos where the limited supply of property to foreigners leaves one other option: the aparthotel. Under the aparthotel system, a non-Swiss can buy a suite in a hotel which he may use for a part of the year, but which he must offer, under contract, for letting through the hotel for the remainder of the time. By law, the hotel must have use of the suite for a minimum of 150 days a year. The hotel is responsible for the maintenance and management of the suite, and can usually guarantee the owner an annual return on investment of between 3 and 5 per cent, depending on how long and at what time of year it is available for let.

The majority of aparthotels offer the equivalent of a hotel room with a bath and small kitchenette; some offer an extra one or two bedrooms. For pure investment purposes the aparthotel is an attractive option, with returns on investment usually higher than if the buyer handled the letting himself. One of the major problems, however, is the usage permitted to the individual owners. Different aparthotels impose different restrictions on when the suite is made available to the owner, but it should be appreciated that to achieve higher rental returns the accommodation must remain available for let in, rather than out of, season.

Buying

Having made a decision to buy a property in Switzerland, a mutually agreeable notary is appointed to act for both parties to ensure the vendor has title to sell the property and the buyer has the necessary funds or mortgage in place. Developers will usually recommend a notary familiar with their particular properties, but the buyer is free to choose any notary he wishes.

A deposit will then be payable to secure the property, and the necessary applications made to the local canton and to the Federal Commission in Berne. As soon as the purchase application is granted, usually within six to eight weeks, the property deed is issued and registered and the appropriate payments of the purchase price and notary's fees are made.

The total legal costs of purchasing vary depending on the registration charge in the canton you are buying. In Vaud, for instance, the total cost is around 5 per cent; in Valais, just 2½ per cent.

Thereafter, an annual tax based on the value of the property is payable to the commune, the canton and the Swiss government. The total sum of this tax is dependent upon the income and worldwide capital assets of the owner, but is usually in the region of 1 per cent of the value of the property. Annual running costs of an apartment, covering maintenance, gardening, snow clearing, water, heating, administration and insurance usually amount to between 0.8 and 1 per cent of the value of the property.

Selling

Provided you don't want to sell up in a hurry, there are few problems associated with selling in Switzerland. As a foreigner you are free to repatriate the proceeds of the sale, including the profit, although you will be subjected to capital gains tax of 18 per cent. It is, however, possible to offset against CGT any money spent on improving the property and the expenses involved in the sale.

Austria

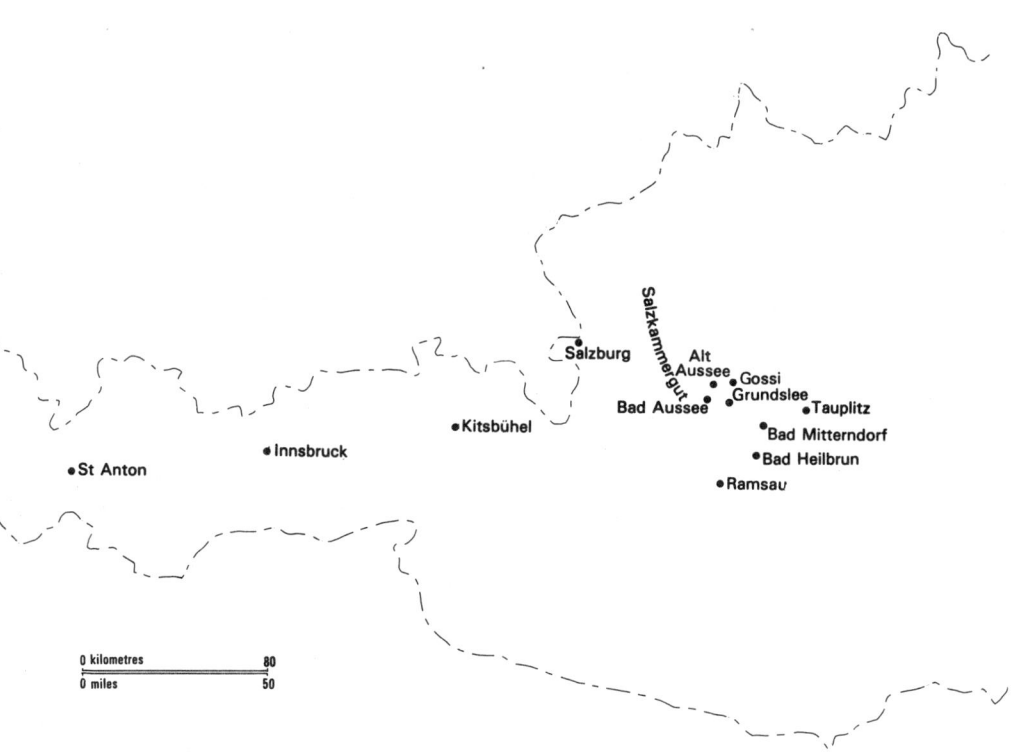

Skiers who dream of buying a picturesque chalet in popular Austrian ski resorts such as Kitzbühel or St Anton will be disappointed. As in Switzerland, restrictions imposed on foreigners prohibit them from buying properties in certain regions, including the two best-known holiday areas, Vorarlberg and the Tyrol. The reason is purely environmental. The Austrians are convinced conservationists and have no wish to spoil their beautiful country with overbuilding, particularly when those buildings might stand empty for a large part of the year.

However, these restrictions do not rule out the possibility of buying property in Austria altogether. A few areas still allocate holiday homes to foreigners, offering the opportunity to invest in this neutral, friendly country where the rate of inflation is the lowest in Europe and yet property values rise steadily year by year. One beautiful region of Austria where that dream chalet can still be bought is the Styrian Salzkammergut.

Salzkammergut

In the heart of Austria, east of Innsbruck and south of Salzburg, the Salzkammergut is known as the Alpine Garden of Austria or Austria's Lake District. It is an area of unspoilt natural beauty with snow-capped mountains, pine-clad valleys and sparkling lakes. Older generations will recognize it as the setting for the operetta *White Horse Inn*, while others will connect it more readily with the film *The Sound of Music*.

The Salzkammergut has been popular with tourists for over a hundred years, both winter and summer. With skiing centred around Schladming and the Tauplitzalm snowfield, the area has hosted the World Alpine Ski Championship and the Ski Jumping World Cup, as well as the World Cup downhill races. From 1990 another range of mountain peaks known as the Loser will come into prominence with newly acquired World Cup status. In the summer, it's possible to ski before lunch on the Dachstein glacier, then windsurf or sail in the afternoon, or have a round of golf. The region is easily accessible either by flying to nearby Salzburg, or else to Munich a two- or three-hour drive away.

A substantial and varied selection of apartments and chalets can be picked up at quite reasonable prices, although because of the scarcity of opportunities to build a brand-new home almost all the properties available are resales. You can choose between properties in the skiing villages of Tauplitz and Ramsau, or else by the lakeside in villages such as Grundsee, Gossl and Alt Aussee. Nowhere is more than a few minutes' drive from the ski slopes. Alternatively you could choose one of the spa towns favoured by tourists since early Victorian times, such as Bad Aussee, Bad Heilbrunn or Bad Mitterndorf. A fully furnished one-bedroomed apartment, for instance, in a development with swimming pool and sauna, ten minutes' walk from Bad Mitterndorf, could cost around £38,000. Alternatively, a ski chalet tucked up in the mountains amidst pine trees, two minutes from the ski lift, costs £75,000. Apartment or chalet, all the properties are built in traditional style.

Salzkammergut

1 bed apartment	£25,000–45,000
2 bed apartment	£30,000–70,000
2 bed chalet	£60,000–80,000
3 bed chalet	£75,000–130,000

Buying

The first procedure for buying an apartment or chalet is to sign an undertaking to buy, signed either in Austria or in Britain. This will be written in German with an English translation, a copy of which is supplied to the purchaser.

A local lawyer acts for both buyer and seller, as is common in many European countries. He is instructed to draw up a contract, with power of attorney to act on behalf of the purchaser, and arrange a mortgage agreement where finance is required. No deposit is usually required.

The next step is normally to sign the completed legal document before an official of the Austrian Embassy in London. The documents and payment are then returned to the lawyer and the money placed in a trustee account in Austria. Having completed these formalities, the buyer is then given the key to the property.

The final stage is to register the title of the property at the land registry. This normally takes four to six months. When registration is complete, payment of the appropriate taxes and fees is required. These amount to 3½ per cent ground buying tax, 1 per cent for an entry fee in the land registry and about 3 per cent to cover trustee management of the money by the attorney/notary. When the sale is completed, the money in the trustee account is released to the seller.

Selling

If and when you decide to sell a property in Austria, there will be no problems repatriating the proceeds including any profit made. Capital gains tax is only payable if you sell within five years of purchase.

CHAPTER 14
COSTS

It is a hard, uncompromising fact of life that most pleasurable and worthwhile achievements require a degree of hard work, self-sacrifice and expense in both time and money. Even the most stimulating and thrilling careers have their tedious, downright boring administrative sides; even the most joyous of marriages have to be worked at. When it comes to buying a property, at home or abroad, the sacrifice that has to be made is in your bank account.

A mistake all too commonly made is to rush headlong into buying a dream cottage or villa in the sun without first working out the incidental costs involved. The price tag might well be affordable, but what about legal fees, agency fees, registration taxes, maintenance, insurance and rates? This chapter details any likely expenses to be incurred, both before and after you receive the keys to the door, as well as ways of covering the costs.

Legal fees and transfer taxes

The first myth to be destroyed is that transfer taxes and legal fees in fellow EC countries must be around about the same as in the United Kingdom. They are not. They vary, of course, from one country to another, but generally transfer taxes alone are between 5 and 10 per cent of the purchase price, compared with 1 per cent stamp duty in the UK. On top of this there will be notarial fees of between 1 and 2½ per cent, and legal fees. The exception to the rule is Andorra, where the total transfer costs, including notary's fees, are normally between 1½ and 2 per cent.

Agency fees

As in Britain, agency fees are not usually something to worry about until you come to sell a property. However, in France the rules vary from region to region: in some areas the seller pays the agency fees, and in others the buyer. It is worth checking whose liability it is before committing yourself to purchase; sometimes you will find that it is included in the asking price. Agency fees in France range between 4 and 8 per cent, again considerably higher than in the UK. In Spain they could be as much as 10 per cent. Generally agents' fees are proportionately more expensive for smaller, cheaper properties.

Running costs and community charges

It would be quite possible to buy a rustic cottage in the Umbrian hills, tap water from a well and forget electricity in favour of oil lamps. The running costs would be virtually zero. Alternatively, you could buy a smart villa on the Côte d'Azur and pay a fortune just on the upkeep of the swimming pool. It hardly needs saying that running costs will vary enormously depending on the type of property, where it is, and, in the case of properties on developments, the extent and quality of communal facilities on offer.

In Spain, a developer is obliged by law to initiate the formation of a community of owners. Each owner has a percentage interest in the community and is liable for community charges on a pro rata basis. This applies whether you have an apartment, a townhouse or a villa.

In an apartment block, for example, the charges may cover lift maintenance and repairs, cleaning, communal electricity, maintenance of a pool and communal gardens and perhaps a day or night porter or security guard. Should you own a villa, then private garden and swimming pool maintenance usually becomes your own responsibility, but you will still be liable for maintenance of roads on the development, street lighting, maybe communal sports facilities and so on.

Annual community charges on a small two-bed unit in an apartment block may be as little as £200–300. On the other hand, community charges on a penthouse in a luxury development with large staff and extensive communal facilities may cost £1500 a year.

Community charges are payable on developments throughout Europe. They will vary depending on the cost of labour in different countries, as well as the amenities on offer.

Rates

Much lower in most European countries than they are in Britain, in some countries rates don't exist at all. In Malta, for example, you get off scot-free, and in Greece there is a one-off payment only if there happens to be a fire service in the region where you are buying a property.

In Ireland, an annual residential property tax of 1½ per cent of the value of the property is only payable if the property is worth over IR£74,300, and then only if your gross household income is over IR£25,800 a year. Rates in Cyprus are rarely over £50 a year, and in Italy rarely over £100 a year. In France they vary from area to area but are unlikely to exceed £100 a year unless you buy in a city or on the Côte d'Azur. In Spain, too, rates are far lower than in Britain; for a two-bed apartment, for example, they might be around £40 a year, depending on location. Rates in Portugal are determined by the estimated rental value of the property, like the system currently being phased out in Britain in favour of a poll tax. For several years rates were kept very low, but in 1988 they virtually doubled in line with several years' inflation. Rates for a one-bedroomed apartment in a desirable coastal location on the Algarve can now be around £120 per annum.

Water and electricity

Connection charges and water and electricity bills thereafter have to be budgeted abroad, just as they do at home. In some countries property owners are expected to buy water and electricity meters and, in the case of new properties, pay to bring such connections to the plot or apartment. You should be particularly conscious of this if your intention is to renovate a rural property miles from the nearest village; the cost of connecting water and electricity could be astronomical.

The method of payment for water and electricity varies from country to country. Water may be included in the general rates, charged as a separate bi-monthly bill, or, as in France, charged just once a year. Electricity consumption is unlikely to be as high in sunny climes as it is at home, but in some countries the cost per unit may well be higher. In Spain, for instance, there is a minimum bi-monthly charge payable whether or not you are resident at the time. For an apartment, this may be approximately £20 a month.

Furnishing

You may be lucky enough to buy an apartment or villa already furnished. Alternatively, if you buy on a new development you may be offered, at the time of purchase, a choice of furnishing 'packages'. The quality of these will vary with the quality of the development, but generally will be better value than if you purchased the individual items yourself. Buying furniture yourself may, of course, be the only option, in which case, if the property is only intended for holiday use, it's probably best to pick up local furniture at local prices. Cheap wicker tables and chairs may not be your first choice at home, but in a sunny climate can be both practical and attractive.

If your intention, on the other hand, is to move abroad permanently, then the whole matter of furnishing has to be looked at more seriously. Many expatriates, even on two-year contracts, have sorely regretted not transporting their familiar bits and pieces with them. Going native is one thing, but not necessarily behind closed doors of what is to become your permanent home.

The only advice here is not to be tempted to cut costs by undertaking the removal yourself. Hiring and loading up a van will be the least of your problems compared with the necessary paperwork involved. If you are the capable type – quite able and willing, for example, to undertake your own conveyancing on buying a house – then, fair enough, you will probably be quite happy dealing with the complex rules and regulations governing international transportation. Otherwise, call in the professionals.

Estimated costs of moving the contents of a small and large family house to various destinations in Europe are shown in the table below. On top of this, you should allow for the cost of insuring your goods while on the road.

	Small family home £	Large family home £
Northern France	500–1000	2250–2750
South of France	800–1100	2500–3000
Switzerland	600–1000	2250–2750
Italy (Tuscany)	750–1000	2600–3100
Portugal (Algarve)	750–1000	2800–3300
Spain – north-east	800–1100	2500–3250
Spain – south-east	900–1200	2750–3500
Balearics	1400–1800	2750–3250
Tenerife	800–1200	2700–3200
Lanzarote	1500–2000	3200–3400
Fuerteventura	1500–2000	3100–3400
Ireland	500–1000	2000–2500
Cyprus (Limassol)	700–1000	1900–2400
Malta	800–1100	2600–3100
Greece (Athens)	700–1000	2000–2500
Turkey (Istanbul)	1500–2000	2500–3000

Prices compiled by Pickford Removals Ltd, to be used for general guidance only.

The British Association of Removers (BAR), based at 3 Churchill Court, 58 Station Road, North Harrow, HA2 7SA, will be able to provide you with a list of firms specializing in overseas removals, and offer some useful tips to make the move as smooth as possible. What's more, the Association can guarantee that, should one of its affiliated companies fail to perform the services you've paid for, the removal will either be completed at no extra cost or your money returned.

Insurance

Earthquakes, you might think, aren't a serious enough threat to worry about. In Greece, however, and in parts of Italy the risk is considered real enough to push up the premiums on buildings insurance. Elsewhere in Europe the premiums payable will be more or less in line with those in the United Kingdom – depending, of course, on the rebuilding costs of the apartment or villa.

Contents insurance, again, will be much the same, although the cover may be reduced if the property is left unoccupied for any length of time. It may, for example, only be covered for theft by forced entry.

In an apartment building, insurance to cover rebuilding costs will usually be included in the community charge. It will only be necessary, therefore, to take out additional cover on damage to the interior, contents and third party liability. Cover can be arranged either through a local company, or a British-based company with a subsidiary in your chosen country of purchase.

Local banking arrangements

In order to pay the water, electricity, insurance and so on, it is advisable to open an account with a local bank. In Spain, this is essential since some bills can legally only be paid by direct debit, and in many countries this will be required anyway in order to make the initial purchase of a property. A lump sum should be deposited in this account every so often to cover not just standing orders but also any unseen eventualities. In most countries your UK bank should be able to organize the opening of an account for you.

Travelling

It can be as quick to fly to a villa in southern Spain as it is to drive to a cottage in the Yorkshire Dales. The cost, however, will be considerably more – an obvious point, perhaps, but pertinent nevertheless, particularly if you have a family in tow. France, Ireland, even northern Spain can easily be reached by car, but elsewhere the price of air tickets must be taken into consideration. Air travel will generally be cheaper out of season; and charter flights less expensive than scheduled flights – unless, that is, you stay for more than a couple of weeks, in which case there may be a supplement charge to tip the balance.

Letting your holiday home

You may feel by this stage that your holiday home had better earn something towards its own keep. Letting a property out is, of course, a way of recuperating costs, although it would be a mistake to believe it will cover them in total, particularly if you have interest to pay on a mortgage. The most optimistic annual net return you are likely to make is about 10 per cent of the purchase price; 5 per cent would be a more realistic figure.

If you intend to let your property out there is really only one important criterion to consider: location, starting with the country. This can make the difference between a tidy little income and no income at all. In Cyprus, for example, foreigners are not allowed to let out their properties for financial gain. The same rule applies to many holiday homes in Malta; only villas with swimming pools can be rented out here, and then only if the owner applies for a renting licence costing approximately £590.

In other countries, where you *are* allowed to rent for profit, you will find it far easier to let out an apartment with beach frontage and good accessibility than one tucked away in a back street some distance from the shops, restaurants and bars, and hundreds of miles from the nearest airport. Ski chalets let well, provided they are within easy walking distance of the resort amenities. Golfing apartments are another good bet, as are marina apartments: at Port Grimaud, for instance, in the south of France, a two-bed cottage with mooring can net a weekly income of £500–600. For consistent letting twelve months of the year, nowhere is as good as the Canary Islands.

Another point to consider is whether or not a development is geared up for letting; some offer full letting facilities, while others even offer a guaranteed rental income from your property. If it has no letting facilities, or if you intend to let out a rural property, it's important to employ a reputable agent to manage the letting of the property for you. It's easy to think you can do it yourself; not so easy in practice when it comes to placing ads and changing the linen every week. Remember, too, that as well as management fees there is tax on rental income and insurance to consider.

Mortgages

One of the commonest and simplest ways of raising finance for a second home abroad is to top up an existing mortgage on the security of your property in the UK. Several financial institutions will loan up to 95 per cent of the value of your home in Britain – the value, that is, after deducting the existing loan. If, for example, you own a property worth £80,000, with an existing mortgage of £30,000, you could borrow up to 95 per cent of £50,000 – depending, of course, on your financial status.

Historically, British institutions have been suspicious of providing a mortgage on the security of a property abroad, for the simple reason that the security is then difficult to realize in the event of foreclosure. In the last couple of years, however, a determination to cross frontiers and break down barriers, largely in preparation for 1992 and the single European market, has released several new mortgage schemes on to the market in Europe. The Abbey National, for example, opened a Gibraltar subsidiary in early 1988 to offer mortgages, in sterling, to British property buyers on the Costa del Sol. Loans of up to 60 per cent of the value of the property can be obtained, secured on the Spanish property, at 3 per cent above bank base rates. Also in Spain, the National Westminster Bank has joined forces with the Spanish Banca March and now secures loans on properties bought on the Spanish mainland; not, however, on the islands. It will lend up to 70 per cent of the value of the property, in sterling or any major European currency. In sterling, it charges a variable interest rate of around 2 per cent above bank base rates. In Portugal, Barclays, in conjunction with its Lisbon office, is now able to take the Portuguese property as security. Rates in sterling are 2½ per cent above base.

A determination to be prepared for the single European market has also brought foreign financial institutions across the water to Britain. Compagnie Bancaire, for example, one of France's largest financial groups, recently opened a subsidiary in Surrey. Called UCB Home Loans Corporation, it was originally set up to make inroads into Britain's then booming domestic mortgage market, but has now established an obvious niche lending to Britons wanting to buy in France. Through its French parent company it can arrange everything from the money itself to valuable help in finding local valuers and lawyers – in short a complete purchasing package, called, appropriately, Le Mortgage. The loan, up to a maximum of 80 per cent of the value of the property, is secured on the property in France and paid in sterling. The interest rate charged is 0·5 per cent above UK bank base rates.

It is also possible to raise a bank loan in sterling via a London branch of a foreign bank. Portugal, for instance, is represented in London by Banco Portuguese do Atlantico, Banco Totto & Acores and Espirito Santo. All offer loans in sterling on the security of a property in Portugal. The maximum loan is usually 75 per cent of the value of the property to be repaid over fifteen years, at rates varying between 2 and 4 per cent over base.

Alternatively, you can arrange financing in the country in which you buy a property. The process can be complicated, though, and costly, and you may be limited as to the amount you can borrow. You should beware, too, that although interest rates in some countries abroad may look attractively low, a swing in exchange rates can cancel in a single blow any savings made.

If you are buying a property in a new development, another option may be to borrow through the developer; in Spain, particularly, it is quite common for developers to supply their own credit facilities. This option is the most convenient of all, but may also be the most expensive. Whichever route you take, do seek financial advice and do view it in the context of your overall financial position. It's worth remembering – as if you could forget – that interest payments can go up as well as down. Bear this in mind and you'll be able to relax and enjoy your home abroad to the full.

AGENTS

France

Babet Sales
14 High Street
Godalming
Surrey GU7 1ED
048 68 28525

Barbers
417–429 North End Road
London SW6 1HG
01-381 0112/385 6666

Declan Kelly Group
Old Portsmouth Road
Guildford
Surrey GU3 1LR
0483 69201

Domus Abroad
4 Gardnor Road
Hampstead
London NW3 1HA
01-409 0571

Farrar Stead & Glyn
656 Fulham Road
London SW6 5XR
01-731 4391

French Associates
Robertsbridge House
Robertsbridge
East Sussex TN32 5AN
0580 880599

Hamptons & Sons
6 Arlington Street
St James's
London SW1A 1RB
01-493 8222

Montpelier International
43 Pall Mall
London SW1Y 5JG
01-930 1700

Prudential Property Services
2 Allington Close
Wimbledon Village
London SW19 5AP
01-947 7333

Rutherfords
7 Chelsea Manor Street
London SW3 3TW
01-351 4454

Tavernstar Ltd
Dominic House
171–177 London Road
Kingston-upon-Thames
Surrey KT2 6RA
01-549 9236

Villas Abroad (Properties) Ltd
55 York Street
Twickenham
Middx TW1 3LL
01-891 5444

Whiteway Properties
12 High Street
Knaresborough
North Yorkshire HG5 0EQ
0423 867047

Italy

Babet Sales
14 High Street
Godalming
Surrey GU7 1ED
048 68 28525

Barbers
417–429 North End Road
London SW6 1NX
01-381 0112/385 6666

Brian A. French & Associates
12 High Street
Knaresborough
North Yorkshire HG5 0EQ
0423 865892

Hamptons & Sons
6 Arlington Street
St James's
London SW1A 1RB
01-493 8222

Italian Country Homes Ltd
Kelly House
Warwick Road
Tunbridge Wells
Kent TN1 1YL
0892 515611

Italian Properties
Old Telephone Exchange
Eckingham
Worcestershire WR10 3AP
0386 750133
(Italy: 010 39 75 855 9597)

Rainbow Properties
Kingston House
7 London Road
Old Stratford
Milton Keynes MK19 6AE
0908 567707

Spain

Aer Lingus Espana (Tenerife)
Urbanizacion Puerto Santiago
Carretera General Los Gigantes
Sontiago del Teide (Aptdo. 3)
Tenerife, Canary Islands
010 3422 867428/868188
(London no: 01-569 4646)

Amarilla Golf & Country Club
(Tenerife)
Cornwall Buildings
45 Newhall Street
Birmingham B3 3QR
021-233 1117

Alexanders (C. del Sol, C. Blanca,
Menorca, Mallorca, Tenerife)
174 Edmund Street
Birmingham B3 2HD
021-236 4422/0874

Babet Sales Ltd
14 High Street
Godalming
Surrey GU7 1ED
048 68 28525

Beaches International Property
(C. Blanca)
3/4 Hagley Mews
Hagley Hall
Stourbridge
West Midlands DY9 9LQ
0562 885181

Beach Villas (C. Blanca, Mallorca)
55 Sidney Street
Cambridge CB2 3QR
0223 353222/350777

Bendinat (Mallorca)
Collier House
163–169 Brompton Road
Knightsbridge
London SW3 1HW
01-589 4567

Binibella Ltd (Menorca)
99 High Street
Kensington
London W8 5ED
01-937 2824

Bovis Abroad (La Manga Club)
62 Brompton Road
London SW3 1BW
01-225 0411

Bradley and Vaughan Overseas
Ltd (C. del Sol, C. Blanca,
C. Brava)
34–36 The Broadway
Haywards Heath
West Sussex RH16 3AL
0444 412551

British Overseas Property Brokers
(C. Blanca)
14a Chine Avenue
Bitterna
Southampton SO2 7JF
0703 443730

Britannia European Property Sales
Ltd (C. del Sol, C. Blanca,
Mallorca, Tenerife)
129 High Street
Henley-in-Arden
Warwickshire B95 5AU
05642 3237

Canary Island Properties
(Tenerife)
46 Victoria Road
Surbiton
Surrey
01-390 7587

Casitas Classiques (C. del Sol)
Berkeley House
121 Foxley Lane
Purley
Surrey CR2 3HR
01-668 5555

Castillo Sur (Tenerife)
Avd Suecia Ed, Avenida
Los Cristianos
Arona 38008
Tenerife, Canary Islands
010 34 22 792319

Catalan Property Services
(C. Brava)
Well House Yard
Hare Street
Buntingford
Hertfordshire SG9 0EQ
076 389 224

Chilcott White & Co. (Tenerife)
125 South End
Croydon
Surrey CR9 1AR
01-688 4155

Compass Estate Agents
(Andalucia)
142 Rose Street
Edinburgh EH2 3JD
031-225 5166

Coope & Co (Properties) Ltd
(C. del Sol, C. Brava, Mallorca,
Menorca)
66/67 High Street
Lymington
Hampshire SO41 9AL
0590 77971

Costa Blanca Villas (C. Blanca)
13–17 Newbury Street
Wantage
Oxfordshire OX12 8BU
02357 65305/72345

David Scott International
(C. del Sol, C. Blanca,
Lanzarote)
Deerhurst House
Epping Road
Roydon, Harlow
Essex CM19 5RD
027979 2162

Difora Benelux BV
(Fuerteventura)
P.O. Box 1123
Southbury Road
Enfield
Middlesex EN2 8DW
01-367 9286

Dominion International plc
(C. del Sol,
Dominion Beach)
Dominion House
49 Parkside
London SW19 5NB
01-946 5522

Domus Abroad (Ibiza)
4 Gardnor Road
Hampstead
London NW3 1HA
01-409 0571

East Midlands Overseas Owners
  Ltd (C. del Sol, C. Blanca,
  C. Brava, Mallorca, Menorca,
  Tenerife, Lanzarote)
774a Mansfield Road
Nottingham NG5 3FH
0602 200259

Euro Property Advisors
  (C. del Sol)
27a New Street
Salisbury SP1 2PH
0722 330847

Fincas La Isla (UK) (Menorca)
Willow Bank House
Higham
Bury St Edmunds
Suffolk IP28 6PA
0284 810153

Fincasol Ltd (C. del Sol)
4 Bridge Street
Salisbury
Wiltshire SP1 2LX
0722 411644

G.D. Properties (Mallorca)
Nightingale House
1–7 Fulham High Street
London SW6 3JH
01-384 1170

Golf del Sur (Tenerife)
Unit A 15 Trinity Business Centre
305/9 Rotherhithe Street
London SE16 1EY
01-232 0121

G.M.G. Properties (Menorca)
22(c) Bridge Street
Pinner
Middlesex HA5 3JF
01-868 5144/429 3813

Gran Sol Properties (C. Blanca,
  Tenerife)
Heatley Street
Preston
Lancashire
0772 25587

Grupo Glomond S.A. (Ibiza)
Can Peter
Santa Eulalia del Rio
Ibiza
010 34 71 33 06 27/33 19 54

Hamptons International plc
  (C. del Sol, C. Blanca)
6 Arlington Street
St James's
London SW1A 1RB
01-493 8222

Homes in the Sun Ltd (C. Blanca)
16 Montague Street
Kettering
Northamptonshire
NN16 8RU
0536 84343

Inter Spain Services UK Ltd
  (C. Blanca)
Suite 2, 66–72 High Street
Rayleigh
Essex SS6 7EA
0268 775165

IPI Ltd (C. Blanca, C. Brava,
  Mallorca, Tenerife)
34 Ship Street
Brighton BN1 1AD
0273 774098/724369

Javea Homes Abroad (C. Blanca)
18 Grange Court Road
Harpenden
Herts AL5 1BY
05827 61691

AGENTS 153

Lanzarote Property Consultants
 (Lanzarote)
55 Downside Road
Sutton
Surrey SM2 5HR
01-642 6284

Lions Overseas Properties Ltd
 (Lanzarote)
Lion House
246 Vauxhall Bridge Road
London SW1V 1AU
01-834 8611

Marisol Villas (C. del Sol,
 C. Blanca)
The Stables
Sugworth Lane
Radley
Oxford OX14 2HX
0865 739422

Menorca Country Club (Menorca)
Felix Lane
Shepperton Marina
Shepperton
Middlesex TW17 8NJ
0932 243104

Mintegui (Mallorca)
Paseo Mallorca, 2
07012 Palma de Mallorca
Baleares
Spain
010 34 71 713944/775484

Miraflores (UK) Ltd (C. del Sol)
116 College Road
Harrow-on-the-Hill
Middlesex HA1 1BQ
01-863 0811

Montpelier International plc
 (C. del Sol)
43 Pall Mall
London SW1Y 5JG
01-930 1700

Nova Leisure Spanish Properties
 (C. Blanca, Tenerife)
27 Promenade
Southport
Merseyside PR8 1QU
0704 36677

The Overseas Property Centre
 (C. del Sol, C. Blanca, Tenerife,
 Lanzarote, Ibiza, Mallorca)
Hilton House
21 The Downs
Altrincham
Cheshire WA14 2QD
061-941 7022

Overseas Residential Property Ltd
 (C. del Sol)
Overseas House
5 Broadway Court
Chesham
Buckinghamshire HP5 1DB
0494 791779

Petersons International (Tenerife)
Corn Street
Witney
Oxfordshire OX8 7DG
0993 771187

PMS Estate Agents Ltd
 (C. del Sol)
48a King Street
Maidenhead
Berkshire SL6 1EQ
0628 776000

Prestige Homes Ltd (C. Blanca)
7 Euston Place
Leamington Spa CV32 4LL
0926 832220

Properties International
Yew Tree House
Dunham Road
Lymm
Cheshire WA13 9UY
0925 75 6723

Prudential Property Services
   (Mainland Spain, Tenerife,
   Lanzarote)
2 Allington Close
Wimbledon Village
London SW19 5AP
01-947 7333

P. & S. Mills Ltd (Almeria)
Castle Mews
29a Castle Street
Salisbury
Wiltshire SP1 1TT
0722 334551

Puerto Sotogrande S.A.
   (Sotogrande)
3 Shepherd Market
London W1Y 7HS
01-491 3665

Robin Knight (Overseas)
   (C. Blanca)
5 Market Place
Harleston
Norfolk IP20 9AD
0379 853907

Russel Cowan (C. Blanca)
38 Albemarle Street
Mayfair W1X 3FB
01-493 5565

Sa Taula Properties (Menorca)
Elm Cottage
High Elms Road
Downe
Kent BR6 7JN
0689 58945

Sol Med Homes (C. del Sol,
   C. Blanca, Tenerife, Ibiza,
   Mallorca, Menorca)
63 Brookhus Farm Road
Sutton Coldfield
West Midlands B76 8QP
021-327 2995

Sturgis International (Marbella)
81 Piccadilly
London W1V 9HF
01-495 3686

Sunshine Associates
   (Fuerteventura)
Weston Green
Thames Ditton
Surrey KT7 0JP
01-398 4746

Tavernstar Ltd (C. del Sol,
   C. Blanca, C. Brava)
Dominic House
171–177 London Road
Kingston-upon-Thames
Surrey KT2 6RA
01-549 9236

Topaz Properties Tenerife
   Ltd (Tenerife)
4 Queens Avenue
Hastings
Sussex TN34 1PA
0424 424008

Vernon Smith European
   (Mallorca, Ibiza)
38 Bell Street
Reigate
Surrey RH2 7BA
0737 246868

Woodside Europa Ltd
   (C. Brava, Lanzarote)
Thetford Road
Ingham
Bury St Edmunds
Suffolk IP31 1NR
0284 84743/8855

Whiteway Properties (Hacienda
   Guadalupe, C. del Sol)
12 High Street
Knaresborough
North Yorkshire
0423 867047

Wimpey Leisure (C. del Sol, Tenerife)
26/27 Hammersmith Grove
Hammersmith
London W6 7EN
01-846 2255

Portugal

Babet Sales
14 High Street
Godalming
Surrey GU7 1ED
048 68 28525

Beach Villas
55 Sidney Street
Cambridge CB2 3JW
0223 353222

Bovis Abroad
62 Brompton Road
London SW3 1BW
01-823 8000

David Scott International
Deerhurst House
Epping Road
Roydon, Harlow
Essex CM19 5RD
027979 2162

Euroactividade
9 Galena Road
London W6 0LT
01-748 4446

Euro Property Advisors
27a New Street
Salisbury SP1 2PH
0722 330847

Eurostat
Merritt House
Hill Avenue
Amersham
Buck HP6 5BQ
0494 724194

Four Seasons Resorts
43 Harwood Road
London SW6 4QP
01-736 0060

Hamptons International plc
6 Arlington Street
St. James's
London SW1A 1RB
01-493 8222

Longcroft Properties Ltd
Compton House
Main Road
Easter Compton
Bristol BS12 3QZ
04545 3351/2

Melody Morgan & Co. Overseas
Chartist Tower Building
8/9 Dock Street
Newport
Gwent NP9 1DX
0633 213351

Montpelier International plc
43 Pall Mall
London SW1Y 5JG
01-930 1700

Overseas Residential Properties
Overseas House
5 Broadway Court
Chesham
Buckinghamshire HP5 1DB
0494 791779

Pine Cliffs Algarve Promotions Ltd
Thames Wharf Studios
Rainville Road
London W6 9HA
01-385 3344

Prudential Property Services
2 Allington Close
Wimbledon Village
London SW19 5AP
01-947 7333

Sande Groupe UK
P.O. Box 170
Amersham
Buckinghamshire HP7 0RU
0494 713920

Sturgis International
81 Piccadilly
London W1V 9HF
01-495 3686

Trafalgar House Residential
  (Europe) Ltd
1 Portland Square
Bristol BS2 8RR
0272 425001

Greece

A. P. Bushell & Co
Peckwater House
Eddystone Road
Thurlestone
Kingsbridge
Devon TQ7 3NU
0548 560370

Robert Comins
2 Market Street
Saffron Walden
Essex CB10 1JB
0799 22641

Properties International
Yew Tree House
Dunham Road
Lymm
Cheshire WA13 9UY
0925 75 6723

Vladi Private Islands
Ballindamm 7
D-2000 Hamburg 1
West Germany
010 49 40 338989

Whiteway Properties
12 High Street
Knaresborough
North Yorkshire HG5 0EQ
0423 867047

Cyprus

Cybarco Ltd
Cybarco House
6 Drama Street
P.O. Box 1653
Nicosia, Cyprus
Nicosia 458058

Leptos UK Ltd
555 Green Lanes
London N8 0RL
01-340 8096

Properties International
Yew Tree House
Dunham Road
Lymm
Cheshire WA13 9UY
0925 756723

Prudential Property
  Services
2 Allington Close
Wimbledon Village
London SW19 5AP
01-947 7333

Whiteway Properties
12 High Street
Knaresborough
North Yorkshire HG5 0EQ
0423 867047

Turkey

Bingham & Elliot International
94 New Kings Road
London SW6 4LU
01-736 6187

AGENTS 157

Tavernstar Ltd
Dominic House
171–177 London Road
Kingston-upon-Thames
Surrey KT2 6RA
01-549 9236

Turkish Properties and Rentals
 Ltd
57 Grosvenor Street
London W1X 9DA
01-355 4068

Whiteway Properties
12 High Street
Knaresborough
North Yorkshire HG5 0EQ
0423 867047

Malta

Association of Estate Agents
P.O. Box 18
Sliema
Malta
010 356 336348

Frank Salt Real Estate Ltd
2 Paceville Avenue
Paceville
Malta
010 356 337373/336175/338775

Malta Property Consultants Ltd
Pinecroft House
22 Vicarage Hill
Farnham
Surrey GU9 8HJ
0252 725446

Andorra

Centuria 21
Avgda Meritxell, 104
Andorra la Vella
Principat d'Andorra
010 33 628 25822/25597

CISA Andorran Properties Ltd
12 Kings College Road
Ruislip
Middlesex HA4 8BH
0895 621617

Invico Ltd
Broomholm
Langholm
Dumfriesshire DG13 0LG
03873 80818

Ireland

Christopher Stevenson Ltd
Victoria House
Park Way
Newbury
Berkshire RG13 1EE
0635 528585

Knight Frank & Rutley
20 Hanover Square
London W1R 0AH
01-629 8171

Patrick James & Co
20 Upper Merrion Street
Dublin 2
0001 761092

Ski Resorts

Beaches International Property
 (France & Switz)
3/4 Hagley Mews
Hagley Hall
Stourbridge
West Midlands DY9 9LQ
0562 885181

Domus Abroad (Switz)
4 Gardnor Road
Hampstead
London NW3 1HA
01-409 0571

Gerard Henry & Co (Austria)
Broomholm
Langholm
Dumfriesshire DG13 0LJ
03873 80818

Hilary Scott Overseas Ltd (Switz)
The Old Bake House
Manor Cottage
Church Lane
Barnham
West Sussex PO22 0BP
0243 554319

Lennards Properties International (Switz)
55 Highview Avenue
Edgware
Middx HA8 9TY
01-958 6976

Mills & Co (France)
The Annexe
The Eades
Upton-upon-Severn
Worcestershire WR8 00N
06846 3921/4588

Osbournes (Switz)
93 Parkway
London NW1 7PP
01-485 8811

Prudential Property Services (France)
2 Allington Close
Wimbledon Village
London SW19 5AP
01-947 7333

Projectel (Switz)
1 St. Omer Ridge
Guildford
Surrey GU1 2DD
0483 571226/68846

Rutherfords (France)
7 Chelsea Manor Street
London SW3 3TW
01-351 4454

Villas Abroad (Properties) Ltd (France & Switz)
55 York Street
Twickenham
Middx TW1 3LL
01-891 5444

LIST OF EMBASSIES

Andorran Delegation in
 Great Britain
63 Westover Road
London SW18 2RF
01-874 4806

Austrian Embassy
18 Belgrave Mews West
London SW1X 8HU
01-235 3731

Cyprus High Commission
93 Park Street
London W1Y 4ET
01-499 8272

French Embassy
58 Knightsbridge
London SW1X 7GT
01-235 8080

Greek Embassy
1a Holland Park
London W11 3TP
01-727 8040

Irish Embassy
17 Grosvenor Place
London SW1X 7HR
01-235 2171

Italian Embassy
14 Three Kings Yard
London W1Y 2EH
01-629 8200

Malta High Commission
16 Kensington Square
London W8 5HH
01-938 1712

Portuguese Embassy
11 Belgrave Square
London SW1X 8PP
01-235 5331

Spanish Embassy
21 Belgrave Square
London SW1X 8UA
01-235 5555

Swiss Embassy
Montagu Place
London W1H 2BQ
01-723 0701

Turkish Embassy
43 Belgrave Square
London SW1X PA8
01-235 5252

ACKNOWLEDGEMENTS

My thanks to the following agents, who assisted in the preparation of this book:

Alexanders
A.P. Bushell & Co
Babet Sales Ltd
Barbers
Beaches International Property
Beach Villas
Bendinat
Bingham & Elliot
Bradley and Vaughan Overseas Ltd
Castillo Sur
Catalan Property Services
Centurial 21
Chilcott White & Co.
CISA Andorran Properties Ltd
Compass Estate Agents
Difora Benelux BV
Dominion International plc
Domus Abroad
Euro Property Advisors
Fincas La Isla (UK)
Fincasol Ltd
Frank Salt Real Estate Ltd
French Associates
G.D. Properties
G.M.G. Properties
Gerald Henry & Co
Hamptons International plc
IPI Ltd
Italian Country Homes Ltd
Italian Properties
Javea Homes Abroad
Keane Mahoney Smith

Lanzarote Property Consultants
Lennards Properties International
Leptos UK Ltd
Lions Overseas Properties Ltd
Malta Property Consultants Ltd
Menorca Country Club
Mills & Co
Mintegui
Montpelier International plc
Osbournes
The Overseas Property Centre
Overseas Residential Property Ltd
Petersons International
PMS Estate Agents Ltd
Projectel
Properties International
Prudential Property Services
Puerto Sotogrande S.A.
Rainbow Properties
Robert Comins
Rutherfords
Sa Taula Properties
Sol Med Homes
Sturgis International
Sunshine Associates
Tavernstar Ltd
Turkish Properties and Rentals Ltd
Vernon Smith European
Villas Abroad (Properties) Ltd
Woodside Europe Ltd
Whiteway Properties